Force Under Pressure

Force Under Pressure
How Cops Live and Why They Die

by Lawrence N. Blum, Ph.D.

Lantern Books
A Division of Booklight Inc.

2000
Lantern Books
One Union Square West, Suite 201
New York, NY 10003

Copyright © Lawrence Blum 2000

Printed in the United States of America

Library of Congress Cataloging-in-Publication Data

Blum, Lawrence.
    Force under pressure: how cops live and why they die / by
    Lawrence Blum.
        p. cm.
    Includes bibliographical references.
    ISBN 1-930051-12-3 (pbk. : alk. paper)
      1. Police psychology. 2. Police-Mortality. 3. Police-Job
      stress. I. Title.

HV7936.P75 B58 2000
363.2'01'9–dc21   00-058365

To Paula, Noah, and Nicole Blum, the best pals a guy could have; and to the memory of Bubba Lu, Sadie, and Bea. Hey, Ma. Hope you can see that I did this.

Acknowledgments

I have a simple definition of a hero. The word describes a man or woman who knows that they could be harmed or killed if they engage some dangerous circumstance, and yet they do so to take care of someone they do not even know. Guess what that makes law enforcement officers. But heroes sacrifice their own well being for others. Hence the motivation for a book to help the heroes stay well, strong, and victorious, became this labor of love. God bless them.

It has been a long road to this book's completion. I had to learn and create new methods to perform my work as a police "shrink," because the stuff I learned in my training as a psychologist was often inapplicable to the injuries suffered by the police officers I was responding to. I had great help and friendship given to me by too many police people to mention here. They know who they are and know that I respect the heck out of them.

James D. Harris, Los Angeles County Sheriff's Department, Retired, partner and friend, taught me a great deal about the promise that is made and must be kept amongst those who work in law enforcement: "If you need me, I will be there for you. I will risk injury or death to get to you, because that is my promise." Sergeants Ed Deuel, R.K. Miller, Herb Cuadras, all of the Huntington Beach Police Department, showed me just how much honor, integrity, courage, and pizzazz, is possible in contemporary police work. Lieutenant Louie Hernandez (Ret.) of the Pomona Police Department opened my eyes and changed my life when he introduced me to weightlifting for strength and mastery. No greater quest exists for police officers than the achieving of mastery.

There were and are Chief Executives of Police Departments who trusted me to create a bridge between what I know and what they know, such as Don Forkus of the Brea Police Department, Don Burnett of the Pomona, San Bernardino, and Palm Springs Police Departments, Steve Simonian of the Montebello and Bell Gardens Police Departments, Ron Lowenberg of the Cypress and Huntington Beach Police Departments, Lee Dean of the San Bernardino Police Department, and Dave Bejarano of the San Diego Police Department. I would follow these people into Hell's mouth. They stand for something I find very honorable.

I thank the California Narcotics Officers Association for allowing me to contribute in whatever small way I can to assist their efforts to support, train, and educate the working police officer.

I thank all of the tactical experts who have spent the past thirty years in the tortuous but critically important task of learning the lessons burned in from the felonious murder of police officers. Captain Richard Wemmer, Los Angeles Police Department, Lieutenant Felix Osuna, Santa Ana Police Department, spent patient hours with me while they shared their great expertise in Officer Survival Training.

It hasn't always been a negative process. There were a lot of laughs along the way. I thank Sergeant Craig Junginger of the Huntington Beach Police Department for one of the greatest comeback lines ever heard in a psychological debriefing for an officer-involved shooting. He was a motor officer, dressed in the heavy and tight pants, high and stiff boots, heavy jacket, and all the sundry equipment a police officer wears when he or she patrols on a motorcycle. He had just survived a life-threatening and grave combat with an armed bank robber. I wanted to get him to express his likely feelings of fear or momentary helplessness when he ran out of ammunition and the crook began to advance on him. I said to him: "Boy, it must have been real hard to move tactically in all of that heavy gear…it could easily make it difficult to respond to the suspect."

"Yes," he said. "But I look so very good in them."

I thank Officer Stacy Lim, Los Angeles Police Department, whose experience gives other officers a clear goal to reach for. Her experience is documented in Chapter 3.

I thank the working police officer, because you all will never know how many of the good people you have saved.

Table of Contents

Introduction:
How Cops Live and Why They Die

I have a recurring dream that plays to me in my sleep. I dream that no more police officers are feloniously murdered, that no more police officers will fall victim. Then I wake up.

It all seems so simple. Police officers are trained from the first day of training at the Academy in the tactics and demeanor they need to stay alive in street encounters. They are trained that officers are to remain in control at all times, because control will enable them to overcome any and all situations they encounter. The message is clear: Take command, *be absolutely certain of that command*, and you will be victorious. Then why does it happen? Why do cops die?

For many police officers, the donning of their uniform, body armor, and the image projected to the world serve to form a protective shield. This shield is needed to protect officers against a bombardment of frustration, pain, and suffering they will encounter on a daily basis. The shield enables officers to function efficiently with no lapses in control and gives them the ability to impact every situation they are called upon to handle. The very survival of the officer requires the maintenance of this control. The fact is emphasized over and over again from the first day of Academy training.

1

And yet, many officers do not survive. Some are shot down by an assailant's bullet. Others are killed, maimed, or crippled in traffic collisions. Others die of heart attacks, liver damage, kidney failure, or strokes. Still others take their own lives in the throes of anger, hurt, and helplessness or do not last the twenty or thirty years needed for a service retirement. They are injured—either by some visible, physical wound they can point to as an explanation for why they can't be a cop anymore, or, in the worst case scenario (to the officer), they are hurt by a psychological wound in which there are neither entry nor exit scars. In these cases, there is nothing to point to and say: "See, here is why I can't do it anymore....Here is why I'm not a cop anymore."

If police officers reading this think back to the moments just before they made their first arrest, they will likely recall that they felt nervous, insecure, and fearful that they might not be tactically or physically up to the task. Then they may also remember that after they made the arrest, their insecurity and fear was replaced by euphoria. The change came about because they used a mental command tool, which can be described as the absolute certainty that the perpetrator was *going to jail!* That perpetrator may have been physically stronger than the officer and of greater physical stature, but the officer always won. At least that's the way it was supposed to happen.

Officers Down...

On October 9, 1990, at 4:30 a.m. (a Monday morning, on early morning or "graveyard" watch), a "911" call came in to the police department. The reporting party (RP) identified himself as a store employee, and told the dispatcher that masked men were holding him hostage and robbing the store. Some additional conversation occurred between the alleged store employee and the dispatcher, when the RP suddenly stated: "I can't talk anymore, they're watching me....I've got to go." The telephone line went dead.

That particular morning, as on most Monday mornings at 4:30, things were quite slow. So slow, in fact, that the watch commander was able to send home two of the six units early. One of the officers still on duty was working on his normal day off to cover for two of his buddies who were recovering from moderate injuries sustained in a traffic collision. He had two years' experience as a police officer. Another was a probationary officer, with approximately eight months on the job. The other two officers were veterans of several years.

The call went out as a possible armed robbery with hostages, at a large warehouse. The officers responded to the call. They were not sure as to what they had: Was this a burglary? Was the gas station at the corner of the parking lot at the store also being robbed? Was this a good one? Were store employees being held hostage? There was some degree of uncertainty as the four officers took positions in the parking lot of the business and began their search of the area.

Mike, the most senior on-scene officer, had wheeled his unit to the far corner of the parking lot, directly adjacent to the front wall of the store, approximately twenty yards from the large front window. He positioned himself along the wall, and carefully approached the window as the other three officers were moving from their different positions. As he reached the edge of the window along the wall, he peered into the store and put out a chilling report: "I've got three bad guys in the store....They're wearing flak vests, ski masks, camouflage suits....They've got 'handy talkies,' and they have AK47 assault rifles. They're holding a number of people hostage. I think they saw me!"

As the other officers heard this report, and noted their partner's tone of voice, they advanced closer to the front of the store to aid Mike. One of the officers, Joe, took a position along the right side, and in front, of a van parked in the lot approximately twenty yards on the near side of the store entrance. Another officer, Peter, took a position on the left side and behind the van. Still another officer was advancing parallel to the front of the building, from the left to the right.

Without warning, the door to the van opened. A man wearing a flak vest, ski mask, and camouflage suit emerged with an AK47 and began to fire automatic bursts at the officers.

Joe, the officer immediately to the front of the van, took four rounds in the buttocks and lower back. Peter took one round in his thigh and one that lodged in his body armor at a position which would have pierced his heart had he not been wearing it. (Think of *that* when you don't feel like wearing your vest!) Mike and the fourth officer escaped physical injury.

Both officers fell to the ground while the suspect continued to lace the area with automatic weapons fire. Joe and Peter, the two wounded officers, returned fire in an aggressive manner, even though they were seriously injured. One of the crooks in the van was hit; the suspect who fired retreated; and the van left the area.

No one knew what the remaining suspects in the store were going to do, how many were outstanding, whether store employees had been hit, or what in hell was going to happen next.

Two fire fighters, one of whom was a commanding officer, crawled on his belly to the fallen officers well before the crime scene was controlled. Had the fire fighters not responded, Joe would likely have died. He was in shock, had lost a great deal of blood, and had minimal vital signs when the fire fighters got to him.

Peter was in a state of immediate mental shock and momentary disorientation, caused by the surprise of the unanticipated attack on himself and his fellow officers. He went into a type of shock reaction. He did not remember much of what he did after the initial shock of being struck—although he acted aggressively and bravely against the suspects.

The suspects inside the store now fled from a rear door. None of the store employees had been harmed physically. The police department requested assistance from all neighboring agencies, and they initiated a search for the suspects. The suspects in the van now carjacked a citizen, forced him into the trunk of his car, abandoned their van, and used this vehicle to make their escape. When the carjacking victim sensed that his car was stopped at a traffic signal and because he (accurately) believed he'd be killed if he remained in the trunk, he opened the trunk from the inside, and fled.

Highway patrol officers discovered one of the suspects at the side of a freeway. He was a (completely rehabilitated) parolee. No other suspects were found, although subsequent investigation identified the others when they were killed in other circumstances brought about by their life of crime. The physical incident had ended.

In the Aftermath of Injury
It is at this point that police officers' intense attention paid to the wounds of their own gets complicated. The reasoning goes that because the physical assault has been survived, the wounded officers must be OK. Uninjured officers have to quash the "there-but-for-the-grace-of-God-go-I" feelings and go back to work without feelings of vulnerability or fear of being hurt.

However, while cops may survive the physical wounds they suffer, they may well have been more wounded psychologically than physically. And it is precisely the requirement to say they're *"okfine"* that makes it more difficult for officers to come back from serious wounds and/or injury.

For several days after the incident, fellow officers visited the two officers wounded in the robbery in hospital. A line of cops—all of whom wished the officers well—were outside and inside their hospital room for hours, bringing flowers and cards.

Then, Joe, the officer shot in the back and rectum, began to suffer secondary but severe pain. While he told no one but the "shrink," he was greatly distressed by a feeling of helplessness, a feeling that he was going to die in the hospital. This was brought about by the fact that he felt he could, at least, fight back while lying on the asphalt outside the store. In the hospital, on the other hand, he thought he was dying, and there wasn't anything he could do about it. As well as the first surgery that had saved his life by closing his rectal wound and giving him a colostomy, a second surgery was performed to remove the blood clots that had formed. Now the visitors were few, and he and his wife began the long, silent, and painful period of his recovery.

The younger officer, shot in the leg and vest, was soon discharged from the hospital. Although normally an active person, he found his normal activities were abruptly halted by the pain in his leg and by the fact he was experiencing feelings he had never experienced before. He was depressed, scared, and angry. He was a "veteran" of seven months as a police officer, and was not prepared for the shock he'd experienced when the door to the van opened in the parking lot. He was not allowed to leave his home and was beginning to have only his feelings of depression as companions. No one understood what he was going through. Furthermore, he was certainly not going to communicate to any of his buddies any "wimpy" reactions he might be experiencing. No one could know he believed he was going to die on the asphalt of that parking lot.

For that officer, another unfamiliar thought pattern began to emerge. What was it going to be like when he returned to work? he asked himself. He hadn't even learned yet how to contain a crime scene, and now he'd been shot. Would the next call he went on be the burglar who would shoot him again? It was this concern that began to convert into fear and anger. He began to expect that some crook would try to assassinate him as soon as he returned to work. He wouldn't let them do it, he thought. He would get *them* first.

The older officer, Joe, was now discharged from the hospital. He was greatly distressed by the apparatus attached to his body, and was in severe pain at all times. He felt severe embarrassment at his wounds, and was becoming increasingly frightened by the fact he could neither feel nor move parts of his body. What if I don't get better enough to return to work as a police officer? he thought. What in the world will become of me if I'm not a cop? This self-doubt, however, was minimal when compared with the commitment this officer had to return to work. He knew his life would never be the same again and the period after being released from the hospital was the toughest. He was in constant pain, in great distress, and was reliving the shooting over and over again—even though he expended great effort to remove these pictures and feelings from his mind.

His flashbacks to the shooting took the form of constantly questioning whether he, or the other officers, could have, should have, or would have done anything different. This thinking became an obsession for him in the early days.

Police Officers and the Psychology of Trauma

The experience of intrusive recollections of being injured is commonplace in officers following incidents in which they have experienced feelings of helplessness and something terrible occurs. This feeling of helplessness is so unacceptable to police officers that they consider ways in which they might not have actually "screwed up" if they had used alternative tactics. They try to make sense of how they could have lost control of the incident. Anything, even making mistakes, is better than helplessness.

This type of thinking, however, is of limited use. By it the officer is able to avoid acknowledging that the suspect had control of the incident and can thus avoid the conscious awareness that he or she had failed to command the situation—as the officer was told he or she must always do in order to be a good cop. However, acknowledging momentary helplessness is part of the healing process necessary to extinguish the flashbacks.

Flashbacks are evidence of a rigidified, repetitive perception that is tied to a shocked condition in the brain. The shocked condition occurs in the "fight or flight" process of the brain, which is not under conscious control by the officer. Neurological activity occurring in the "fight or flight" area of the brain is instinctive—fueled by the hormones that mobilize the body for emergency reaction. These hormones prolong the memory of the shocking event, and inhibit memory of any other circumstance.

When an officer's thoughts have been disrupted by trauma, he or she is usually not conscious that the recurring thoughts and feelings he or she is having are actually a memory of the incident. The officer will more likely experience these traumatized perceptions, focus his or her attention on some currently occurring external irritant, project the traumatized perceptions onto the irritant, and believe that the irritant is causing the continuing internal distress. This misplaced irritation occurs because the effects of the hormone noradrenaline—especially the rigid memory-maintained—are instinctive fuels for emergency action and not under the conscious control of the individual.

Through psychological debriefing, a process of conscious analysis is undertaken in which the officer is assisted in acknowledging the momentary, situational helplessness he or she may have experienced during lethal contact. The officer is enabled to understand the source of any sensory, physical, or emotional shock reactions that may have occurred during his or her involvement in the trauma incident. The feeling of shock, helplessness, or loss of control is especially likely to occur if the officer experienced events he or she was not psychologically prepared for.

In the debriefing process, neurological activity is shifted back to the cerebral cortex, where information provided by the senses is processed, conscious control is exerted over the shocked emotion, neurological activity is lessened in the "fight or flight" area of the brain, and the rigidified, repetitive reflex reaction of flashbacks is slowly extinguished. It may sound complicated, but that's how it works.

The Recovery

The younger officer's physical condition improved over a number of months, so it would have been difficult for other officers to perceive the same level of mental concerns about his performance as a police officer as the more seriously wounded officer was having. "What's he got to worry about?" they would have asked. "He's going to return to duty in a few months. Anyway, he's going to get the Medal of Valor, and be treated as a wounded veteran. Hero status! Can you believe it?"

For the younger officer, however, things were different. What is going to be expected of me? he asked himself. How the hell am I supposed to act? No other officer knew he had a constant thought in his mind, namely that there was going to be a burglar who would catch him off-guard and shoot him.

This thought flooded the younger officer's conscious thoughts as he began to recover his physical mobility. The thought—a kind of premonition—was accompanied by two emotions that became his constant companions: fear and anger. By experiencing a premonition, the officer was actually re-experiencing emotions generated at the original moment of impact—something that may occur for months or years after the incident. When this happens, the officer then focuses his or her attention on some current or future concern, experiences the traumatized perceptions, and "plays out" a mental scenario the perceptions create in his or her own mind. This is done to make sense of, or validate, the reactions the officer had back when the incident occurred (but which are being experienced at the present time).

During the first several weeks after his return to duty, the younger officer was preoccupied by this premonition—expecting he was going to be shot and experiencing the feeling he would shoot someone. It was difficult for him to realize that these very real thoughts and feelings were, actually, memories of the exact mental and emotional circumstances that occurred at the moment when he was shot. Later, as he became more familiar with patrol, the fear lessened, as did the premonition (in frequency, if not severity), and he began to become cynical and angered by his perception that other officers did not know what police work was really about. If these officers were newer than he, and could not have possibly imagined what it felt like being shot, he was furious with them: What the hell were they so "fat, dumb, and happy" about!? he thought.

He began to feel resentful of more experienced officers for their thoughtlessness about what he had been going through after being shot. More experienced officers did not want to think about being wounded and, therefore, made comments about him he believed were evidence of their thoughtlessness. A contact was made by a member of a police Trauma Support Team (who had himself been shot) with the more seriously wounded officer. I believed that the wounded officer would feel more comfortable and "normal" about the frustrations of his recovery if he could communicate with other officers who had experienced similar circumstances. This contact resulted in a filmed re-enactment of the shooting for training purposes, an event that provided an emotionally recuperative or "healing" experience for both officers.

The more seriously wounded officer had additional surgery with a neurosurgeon, and it was discovered that his nerves were not severed nor damaged. Rather, the immobility and numbness were caused by scar tissue. He was told that he would, eventually, regain the use of his foot. Still more months went by, and additional surgery removed the apparatus from him, returning his body to its normal functioning. He returned to light duty, put on his uniform again, and left his home each day to go to work, as he said, "just like normal police officers do."

The Result

It has been several years since these two police officers were struck down in the street. How simple it seems to write down, in just a few pages, what these two heroic young men have gone through. How useless words are in communicating the struggle to overcome both the physical and emotional wounds experienced on and after that event. As it is, both officers continue to experience struggles with personal, domestic, and work circumstances that would not have occurred but for the fact they were shot. They continue with their comeback, and will succeed. It is individuals like these two officers who truly embody the phrase "America's finest." They also give evidence to the importance of maintaining a positive mental attitude—the will to survive—during and after lethal contact.

Law enforcement is often reluctant to discuss, support, and train for this critical survival factor. And yet it continues to define those who will survive attacks by criminals and return to a fruitful, full life. It is simple to observe an entry wound scar and see the injury an officer has undergone. It is more difficult, and more unsettling, to acknowledge the emotional scarring that can last for a far longer period of time than physical wounds. The maintenance of a positive mental attitude requires us to acknowledge and conquer feelings that previously were taboo for cops to talk about.

In addition to the (officer safety) causal factor of positive mental attitude, a critical requirement for officers is to eliminate any show of emotion during or after street encounters. The message here is also clear: Any show of emotion and you lose control. The officer soon learns that the ability to eliminate any direct expression of emotion is also of great benefit in allowing him or her to build a type of callus or insulation over emotions that help the officer withstand encounters in extremely distressing situations.

When the cop has to confront the child who is abused, murdered, or dies in a traffic collision or the elderly woman who is knocked down and robbed for the tiny amount in her purse; when the officer sees, instead of the victim's face, the face of his or her own children or spouse or when the dead body wears the same uniform—all of these must be experienced without any loss of control or composure by the officer. The cop must remain immune.

Unfortunately, the calluses don't always work. Many police officers experience severe stress reactions that interfere with their life in the areas of work, family, and personal health. Too many police officers become preoccupied or distracted by frustrations, irritability, or distress, and are killed in the line of duty because they make that fatal error. Still other police officers are forced into medical or stress disability requirements, and lose the dignity and pride of a service requirement.

The Rookie and the Biker

There are many cases that can illustrate the trauma that affects police officers. One in particular involves a Field Training Officer (FTO) and a trainee in the early stages of field training. The FTO (who was driving) and the trainee observed a motorcycle weaving in and out of traffic. The FTO drove parallel to the motorcyclist and ordered him to pull over to the curb. The biker looked at the two officers, extended the middle finger of his hand at them, and accelerated rapidly on the motorcycle. The FTO, a twelve-year veteran, told the young officer, a two-month rookie, to broadcast the pursuit. The rookie complied and did quite well—considering the patrol car screeched around corners with the siren screaming in the rookie's ears. The motorcycle rider continued to goad them by slowing periodically, when he was far ahead of the patrol car, then accelerating quickly to maintain the pursuit.

As the motorcycle turned east on the main thoroughfare with the patrol car behind it, the biker and the twelve-year veteran saw a train across the street two blocks ahead. The motorcycle slowed as the rider anticipated alternate routes around the train. The patrol car was closing ground, and the FTO yelled at the rookie: "We've got him!"

Just as the rider was about to take to the sidewalk to avoid apprehension, he apparently saw the caboose of the train and accelerated, perhaps believing he would successfully cross the tracks at the rear of the train. As the rider of the motorcycle reached approximately 50 mph, it appeared that he then saw there was a double set of tracks and another train was approaching behind the first one, heading in the opposite direction. He began to brake the motorcycle, but it was obvious he wouldn't stop in time.

The biker laid the motorcycle down on its side. With sparks flying from the metal scraping against asphalt and gravel, the motorcycle passed by the rear of the caboose of the first train, and passed cleanly beneath a car of the second train. The rider was not as lucky. He left the motorcycle cleanly but could not stop the forward motion of his body. The wheels of the rolling boxcar severed his body just below the waist and his upper torso was dragged about twenty feet.

The patrol car slid to a halt. The FTO quickly slammed the gearshift lever to park and bolted from the car. The rookie had a bit more difficulty. Everything seemed to be in the way, and he was hung up on the seat belt. Then his holster became pinned between the seat and the rocker molding at the bottom of the door. Finally, he was free of the car and moving toward the FTO, who was standing over the biker.

As the rookie stood by his FTO, he looked down at the severed body. The biker lay on his back looking up at them. Blood was everywhere, flowing from the cavernous opening below his waist. The biker's face was contorted in pain. His mouth opened and closed with a silent scream. To the rookie, the biker's mouth strongly resembled that of a tropical fish. The arms of the biker reached up like those of a small child reaching for its mother.

The rookie now looked into the face that pleaded for unknowable things and looked up at him begging for help. Then the rookie noticed that the intestines of the biker were flowing from the gaping abdominal hole, and a brown and red gruel was oozing over his spit-shined shoes. The rookie then administered the last decree of justice to the biker (who had known various sentences in his life, as it turned out). The last sight the biker took with him from this world was that of the rookie police officer losing his breakfast onto his face.

The rookie became a legend among his peers, and for years was held in high regard by all traffic officers who ever had contact with outlaw motorcycle-gang members. The rookie, later the veteran, would tell stories of the event while having a beer after work with the guys. He would, however, often, on the way home from work, and, occasionally, when the biker would visit him in the middle of a nightmare that has remained with him over a twenty-one-year career, sob and apologize to the biker: "I'm sorry I threw up in your face as you died."

Stories like this epitomize the consequences that can negatively impact the lives of law enforcement officers. Somewhere in the deep recesses of most officers' memory, there is a biker, a baby, or another victim whose injury touches a sensitive nerve that sparks a nagging ache, nausea, guilt, or other distressful reaction. Indeed, the types of incident that haunt a cop—and which can cause damage to their self-esteem, family relationships, and health—are not likely to be dramatic ones, such as an officer-involved shooting. Rather, they tend to be those in which the officer failed to impact or prevent some tragic event to people he or she did not wish harm to come to. When an officer is troubled by uncontrolled emotions, preoccupation and distraction caused by such upset cannot help but compromise an officer's tactics and safety.

The purpose of this book is simple. Officer survival training—while excellent in teaching the use of tactics, weapons, and coordination of action with other officers—may often not include a critical ingredient: maintaining control against the mental and emotional compromise that could disrupt officer-to-officer tactics, officer safety, and officer health and wellness caused by lapses or "freezing" in concentration, judgment, and decision-making. The traditional avoidance in police training of the psychological and physiological impact of police work upon officers must be changed. There now exist simple-to-use methods that ensure that officers continue to maintain their concentration and focus of attention under any and all circumstances.

In some ways police officers treat their emotions a lot like a carpenter treats his or her hands. If one were to examine the hands of a carpenter on the first day of his or her apprenticeship, they would appear soft, unblemished, and uncallused. At the end of several days, those hands would be rough, blistered, splintered, and perhaps bleeding. Of course, six months later, the hands would appear hardened and callused, impermeable to the same elements that wounded them six months earlier. Calluses are the body's protection for the hands. Cops do the same thing with their emotions: they cover them with calluses as a natural defense against the pain they may experience in the course of their duties.

The problem that is created by placing such emphasis on calluses—as opposed to familiarity, practice, command, and control—is that the officer is often not permitted sufficient ventilation or healing for the wounds he or she receives throughout his or her career. Officers have often turned to such aids as alcohol, the discharge of anger towards loved ones, and/or self-defeating or self-destructive behaviors.

Ultimately, injuries to their mental and emotional well-being that are ignored by officers may act like secondary infections that fester and become causes of damage to their life. Extensive research has shown that such patterns of response to the work of law enforcement have resulted in a greater likelihood of sudden-onset coronary death, diabetes, cancer, and thyroid disease—a risk that increases the longer the officer performs his or her work.

There are, without a doubt, at least two "selves" within most cops. "Outer" cops are the officers who graduate from the Academy. They are a damn sight better than anyone else. They handle any situation and always impact that situation for victory. They never show any emotion or lose control. They use command presence in dealings with police matters, as well as in their personal lives. They never lose their service weapon or other equipment in a struggle with a felon. They never ask for help with problems they may be having. They quickly become irritated, angry, and resentful at not being treated with the proper recognition: "Don't they realize what I do?" they ask. "How hard I work? And this is how they treat me?"

The "inner" cops are the persons inside the uniform. They are, in actuality, often extremely sensitive individuals. They care. In no other occupation in the history of the world do individuals sacrifice and deny their own needs for people they don't even know, as do police officers. If you think about it, the act of risking one's own safety and well-being for someone one doesn't even know is a good definition of a hero. But a hero, by definition, sacrifices a part of him- or herself.

The "inner" cops are the ones who feel the pain experienced in encounters with innocent victims. They can experience the helpless feeling of getting there too late to prevent the harm from being done. They want justice. They don't think it appropriate to see a child-abuser or wife-batterer being released on their own recognizance because a jail is crowded. They don't want a prosecuting attorney to refuse to file a case of sexual assault on a ten-year-old developmentally disabled girl because "the victim will not be attractive to the jury." They want promotions to be based on merit and not "juice."

There is a scene in the movie *Platoon* in which a squad is on patrol and has taken an ambush position during the night. A young soldier is seen with a towel over his head, protecting himself from the mosquitoes, as he sits and watches shadowy figures move silently through the darkness. Suddenly, the enemy closes ground with him, there is an explosion, and the screen bursts into a firefight. One of the members of the squad takes a position with the machine gun and begins firing. He is hit by fragments of an exploding grenade and is seriously wounded. He begins to scream in pain and fear. As the firefight ends, the enemy runs back into the bush and there is silence, with the exception of the screaming man. As the squad member lies screaming, the sergeant kneels beside the injured man and clamps his hand over the man's mouth to stifle the noise. He orders the wounded man: "Shut up....Shut up and take the pain." The wounded man ultimately dies.

What the sergeant said in the film is identical to the process cops have gone through from warriors in biblical times to the present day. These people have shut up and taken the pain; they have crammed years of emotional bleeding down deep inside of them, and some of them have died because of it.

There are a variety of reasons for the above process. Society demands it of cops, they demand it of themselves, and their peers demand it. We teach the new cop to behave this way, and it is necessary. No human being can see children murdered, mutilated bodies strewn on the asphalt as a result of traffic collisions, and witness man's inhumanity to man without being moved.

In my clinical and professional experience within law enforcement, three themes appear to influence officer dysfunction or breakdown in family, work performance, personal health, and survival tactics. First, police officers have often been insufficiently prepared for the psychological and physiological reactions they will experience in response to their work. Second, police officers exist in an environment where the message is clear: "If you feel, you cry....If you cry, you can't work....If you can't work, you're losing it....And if you lose it, you can't be a cop anymore." Third, it is probable that officers grew up in environments that strongly influence how they react to problems perceptually, emotionally, and behaviorally; that is, a great many police officers were children of some type of environment where they learned to "stuff it."

The traditional avoidance in police training of the psychological and physiological impact of police work upon officers must be changed. It is not expected that this book, nor the very best in officer survival training, will prevent all further incidents of officers lost in the line of duty. That is a tragedy that will, unfortunately, take more fine heroes before their time. This work is intended to provide bridges to the missing links in Officer Survival Training that can save officers' lives. Further, the preemptive psychological debriefing techniques and officer-wellness tools taught in this book will help officers condition themselves to be victorious psychologically as well as physically. It can save families from unnecessary divorces and provide "the good guys" with a structure to give themselves the care, concern, and relief from psychological and physical wounds that their daily heroics deserve.

1: Officer Survival Training:
Seven Basic Causal Factors

Officer Survival Training, as it is now taught, usually addresses seven basic causal factors. Investigations into hundreds of officer-involved shootings have found one or more of these factors active in over ninety-nine percent of all shootings, some where the cop lived and some where the cop died. These factors are:

1. Developing and using a **tactical plan** to adapt to the many possible circumstances encountered;
2. **Communication** of coordinated actions with other officers;
3. **Avoidance of independent action** or separation of partners when in hot pursuit;
4. Gaining and maintaining **familiarity with equipment**;
5. Using **proper tactics** in response to diverse incidents;
6. Maintaining effective **physical condition** and knowing one's own physical limits; and
7. Keeping a **positive, dominant mental attitude** ensuring the will to survive.

1. Planning

The use of planning is the most consistently taught survival method in police training.

Tactical planning saves lives, and those who have a plan ready for use in case of lethal contact will survive. Traditional uses of planning usually have the officer develop a series of hypothetical scenarios he or she might encounter during a regular tour of duty. The officers then think through the range of possible reactions and/or responses that would be appropriate to any given circumstance encountered—such as their cover, concealment, and positions placing them at an advantage. When they contact a suspicious-looking subject/suspect, they learn to consider how this subject might act from how the subject is reacting to their presence, and what reactions will be best used to command and control the said subject.

The purpose of planning is to ensure that the officer is able to use **proactive** methods of command. Being proactive gives the officer the tactical edge needed to avoid being overwhelmed or surprised by the acts of the subject/suspect, which would have the effect of placing the officer in a defensive, weakened position. Indeed, the ability for police officers to defeat physically superior suspects requires the *absolute certainty* in the officer that what he or she is doing is right, correct, and proper. Such certainty is not possible when the officer encounters unanticipated elements he or she was not psychologically or tactically prepared for. Unanticipated elements shock, surprise, and weaken police officers' thinking, rendering even the most experienced officer vulnerable to trauma and/or defeat. Defeat for a cop can mean his or her death.

Most police readers of this text will likely take for granted that all cops automatically use planning. Police officers learn this tactic and survival factor from day one in the Academy—and have it drummed into them by Field Training Officers (FTOs). However, a problem exists in expecting this factor to be an automatic police tool used by the officer as a reflex action without the need for conscious assessments and purposeful decision-making.

When an officer first begins to learn a new skill or technique, he or she is conscious of every element in the required action. As the officer gains more practice and proficiency in the skill or technique, he or she is less attentive to each detail. The practiced behaviors become familiar to the officer, who is less conscious of each element of the required behavior because she or he requires less concentration to remember all of the things that have to be accomplished. What we do every day becomes familiar to us. What is familiar we perceive as normal, and, therefore, we don't pay as much attention to important elements. For officers, the normal feels good because it allows them to relax somewhat and reduce tensions they may have by using their ability to predict or anticipate what they will encounter at the scene. When officers hear the radio call or penal code number dispatched, they may already be telling themselves: "Oh, it's one of those....This is what I'm going to find when I get there."

Expectations or predictions about what the officer will find may be comforting to the officer, but they lessen the likelihood she or he will take the time to consistently train the mind to make tactical analyses and decisions and develop proactive plans from the body of knowledge they have learned.

2. Communication

The causal factor, **communication**, is critically important for officer safety, survival, and tactical coordination. Without communication, even the best plan will lose a great portion of its value.

Police officers often have real difficulty when it comes to this very important facet of officer survival. I am concerned that we may be "missing the boat" somewhat in not training new, primarily young police officers to obtain skills in purposeful concentration, assessment, and communication—methods they can use to manage subjects and suspects both verbally and nonverbally. The reason why there is a need for concentration and communication skills training is that many recent applicants for police work may not be mentally prepared for what they will encounter as police officers. They

21

probably lived at home with their parents until they became police officers, and, therefore, had probably not faced serious consequences for their actions until the time they pinned on their badge.

The result of the last ten years or so of recruitment has often been a generation of new officers with little in the way of prior life experience to prepare them to confront the range of circumstances they will be expected to manage in police work: family disturbance calls; mentally ill persons (who have been de-institutionalized over the past two decades without viable community resources); substance-involved subjects, who are much more likely to challenge police officers' authority; a population of parolees who are more violent and well armed than ever in the history of law enforcement in this country; a social climate in which there are likely to be pressures to punish the officer for doing his or her job because of media sensationalism; the proliferation of lawsuits; and, finally, the fear of vicarious liability that currently controls policy in most police agencies.

The need for effective mental conditioning and communication skills in police officers has never been greater than it is currently. Knowing how to manipulate or de-escalate emotionally upset or potentially resistant persons keeps the officer in a commanding position, and may save the officer's (and the subject's) life by enabling the officer to "read" the subject and accurately predict what the subject is about to do. Indeed, while the word "manipulation" has a generally negative connotation (implying an insincere purpose in an interaction), it is precisely the ability to manipulate people that will keep an officer safe and in command of a situation. The problem noted here is that it is difficult for an officer to "admit" that he or she could use some assistance in developing skills in maintaining concentration under pressure and communication. There is a great degree of "ego," or self-image, that each officer has invested in his or her work. No one wants to be thought of as a "dumb" cop; or, worse yet, not "one of the guys."

22

Because of this, therefore, few officers are willing to take the initiative of stepping forward to voice an opinion about the best way for an officer, squad, or unit to solve a problem. Few cops want to be the one to tell the undercover officer: "Hey, buddy, this reverse sting doesn't look right...let it go. I don't want you to be killed in a rip-off attempt." No cop wants to be the one to tell another officer: "Hey, buddy, you're driving too recklessly out there. Is there something on your mind? Even though I know you're tactically expert, you've been acting like you're H.U.A. [Head Up Ass] Get on top of it, buddy, I don't want you to die." It is extremely difficult for someone to tell a fellow officer—especially if that officer is senior—that his or her tactics are not safe.

Unfortunately, many good ideas are lost because of the need for tact or diplomacy. Also, many bad ideas or tactics continue to be enacted because nobody wants to challenge the "system." While it is taken for granted that police officers engage in interpersonal communication, many have significant, episodic difficulty in purposeful or manipulative communication. When police officers are troubled, preoccupied, or distracted by problems in their life, their ability to defuse potentially dangerous circumstances can be lessened or lost. Instead of verbally coaxing someone into cuffs, the officer's safety and well-being may be compromised by the uncontrolled impact of whatever is preoccupying or concerning him or her.

Maintaining effective presence of mind and purposeful communication, therefore, is an obviously critical element in tactical activities. The point to be emphasized here, however, is that purposeful concentration and communication serves the officer not only in regard to notifying dispatch or other officers as to his or her location and intent during a tactical encounter. The undertaking of purposeful communication activates the part of the officer's brain *that recognizes threat and the need to shift one's tactics—the part of the brain that is shut down during a "fight or flight" response.* The lack of such concentration and communication has caused impulsive reactions in officers who "leaped before they looked." A person would never dream of diving into a swimming pool without first ascertaining that there was water in it. Why then do officers often "leap" into a foot pursuit or other dangerous circumstance without first ensuring they are in a position of advantage?

In some of these instances, officers have looked up to the heavens and thanked the deity for letting them "skate" this time. In others, the officer has died either by a felon's bullet or by traffic collisions he or she could perhaps have avoided with greater concentration or awareness.

3. Splitting of Police Partners

In the causal factor called splitting of partners it is easy to observe the coexistence of independent action and communication. One of the reasons that police partners split up is an absence of, or dysfunction in, communication. In cases of faulty communication, neither officer knows what his or her partner is going to do in a given set of circumstances. The "leap" into a tactical encounter alone has been one of the greatest killers of law enforcement personnel. There really *is* safety in numbers. Yet law enforcement officers often throw away this tactical edge and challenge the criminal on the criminal's own ground.

A subtle yet important fact that is often ignored even though it stares us in the face is that, in the greater scheme of things, when a criminal sees a police officer there is a primal instinct that causes the criminal to run from him or her. Conversely, the same primal instinct causes the young, aggressive police officer—upon seeing the criminal—to pursue to the point of exhaustion. In pursuit, cops have torn up their uniforms, broken their legs jumping over fences, been bitten by dogs in the middle of the night, and experienced the bright, blinding flash of handguns and shotguns fired at point-blank range. Some have given up their lives and poured their blood onto the broken asphalt of alleyways and back lots because they could not control the immediate impulse to chase the bad guy before their back-up arrived.

While the reality is that most foot pursuits do have probable cause justification, the loss of a police officer killed alone makes this justification seem meaningless.

4. Familiarity with Equipment

Lack of consistent and realistic practice with equipment is a mistake that can happen to any police officer. In a tactical encounter, the brain will engage neural pathways that have been conditioned and practiced. In other words, in the middle of an emergency response, a police officer will do as she or he has practiced over and over again. If this practice has not occurred or if the officer's practice has not been identical to the tactical encounter, the officer's response may be insufficient to withstand a suspect's assault.

Another critical aspect of familiarity with equipment has to do with police officers' traditional tendency to cut corners. As soon as they pass probation, officers often neglect or underemphasize the monthly qualification with their service weapon at the shooting range. Let's face it, while there is obvious benefit to range shooting, standing at the fifteen-yard line at a barricade shooting three shots strong-handed and three shots weak-handed just does not equate to the elements the officer will experience if he or she is involved in a tactical encounter containing moving multiple suspects and lethal threat.

As another example, think for a moment of the high proportion of officers' physical altercations with physically assaultive suspects which begin standing up and then end up on the ground. Then consider the low proportion of police training and weekly practice spent in effective ground-fighting or grappling tactics. It is clear that training in this area does not often enough match the need on the street.

25

5. Proper Tactics

The factor of proper tactics, while discussed in police training, is often one of the most difficult to make consistent among different duty watches, patrol-versus-detective divisions, and different agencies. What must be understood in officer survival training is that officers' mental concentration must be upon the elements of the tactical encounter itself. Officers must be free from any compromised mental activity that may have developed from disturbances in emotion, mood, or judgment. Concentration in the face of threat, danger, or chaos is the one consistent requirement of proper use of tactics regardless of beat, level of activity, jurisdictional character, and/or policy of different agencies.

However, law enforcement's historic avoidance of "psychobabble"—i.e. maintaining intensive concentration and attention during chaos or emergency without disruption from emotion or circumstance—has often prevented proper mental and emotional conditioning and officer wellness from being used as critical components in officer survival training. The depressed cop who kicks a door open with no thought or concern about a possible suspect inside; the officer who doesn't wear body armor because it doesn't feel comfortable; the officer who contacts the suspect too soon because he or she "can't wait" for perimeter containment; the officer who turns his or her back on a car filled with suspicious suspects—all have a consistent theme underlying their improper tactics. This theme is the lack of a dominant, controlled, and well-conditioned mental process and attitude that are required to command, win, and survive any and all tactical encounters.

While mental attitude is, of course, addressed when the concept of officer survival is discussed, the advice usually consists of telling the officer candidate that he or she must have a winning attitude to survive. How the officer is to keep and enhance this attitude is often left up to the individual officer to figure out. Police officers are often unprepared by training for the emotional and physiological reactions they are likely to experience in a trauma call for which they were tactically quite well prepared. Second, officers generally do not properly debrief these emotional and physiological reactions so as to defuse the potential for post-traumatic stress symptoms and subsequent compromise to officer safety and wellness. Third, many agencies have post-incident investigative procedures that isolate the officer, who may be dealt with by investigators using the same procedures applied to suspects. Thus, the shock, distortion in perceptions, and extreme emotions (such as fear, helplessness, and anguish) that an officer may experience during a traumatic event may rigidify in the officer's mind and continue to affect the officer for years.

The tried-and-true police method for dealing with distressing emotions is to pretend they do not exist. The *modus operandi* is to remove the emotions from conscious awareness. That is, the locations in the brain that consciously recognize and label distressing emotions are extinguished, while the automatic tactical response procedures he or she has been trained in allow the officer to function without conscious thought.

While these methods sometimes work well for years, officers will find it difficult to recognize that problems they are having (e.g., escalating calls they used to handle calmly, taking antacid medicines, having reports "kicked back" for errors that they used to write effectively, withdrawing from loved ones, getting citizen complaints for excessive force that the officer never had before) may very well be the tip-off that an officer has been subjected to a traumatic episode or episodes without being adequately debriefed.

It is possible that the experienced police reader will react with a contemptuous statement about today's discussion of cops, mental conditioning, stress, and trauma: "We dealt with all this stuff, what's all this stress crap about?" The primary reason cops generally will not acknowledge that they suffer from post-incident problems is fear they will be seen as inadequate or weak. Admitting fear or helplessness flies in the face of the image of police introduced in the Academy and

27

conditioned in the field. The message is clear: "No good cop loses control. Showing emotion is losing control. No good cop shows emotion."

6. Police Image

The image of the police officer is known well before the recruit graduates from the Academy. Police drama is well publicized—from such early productions as "Dragnet," "The Untouchables," "Highway Patrol," *Dirty Harry*, *Bullitt*, *The French Connection*, etc. More recent productions have attempted to portray a more human side of police work, even while they paint the picture of cops who never lose a fight, never miss what they shoot at, and never lose control of situations they encounter.

The reality of modern police work—where the officer is more afraid of what his or her department, the courts, and/or the media will do to them than afraid of harm from the tactical encounter—is strikingly absent from dramatic portrayals of the law enforcement environment. The 1980s and 1990s were, and the new millennium is likely to be, a tough time for police officers. Media attacks on police actions and "sting" operations against officers assisted by network television have made officers aware they are at risk for doing the job they were trained to perform. Such a paradoxical environment of being trained to always be in control, while actually experiencing feelings of helplessness as well as attacks from the very society they are attempting to protect, will make it difficult for officers to maintain control, health, and well-being in the course of their lives.

There are traditions in police departments used in order to ensure that the new recruit quickly takes on the attributes of the group of officers already there—or the recruit does not long remain in that agency. These traditions serve to provide the blueprint of appropriate behaviors, attitudes, emotional reactions, and personal demeanor. Some of the guidelines that determine the demeanor of the police officer can be seen in the manner in which new officers are treated by more experienced officers. In some agencies, new recruits are involved in social and departmental activities from day one. There tends to be a family atmosphere in these departments, and socialization depends upon the recruit being a loyal son or daughter—feeling and showing appreciation for the support he or she is shown by internalizing the attitudes, values, and behaviors of the more experienced and/or ranking officers.

In other departments, however, new recruits are not spoken to by more experienced officers. They may not be included in social and/or recreational activities, and will not be invited to after-watch "Discussion Clubs." It is made clear to the recruit that he or she will have to earn acceptance and support. The recruit earns this acceptance and support in the field. Recruits quickly learn they must first "make bones," or be victorious, in a dangerous encounter, to prove themselves to be "stand up." They must show no sensitivity nor react in a manner that would compromise their image as a warrior.

7. Field Training

The most consistently powerful vehicle of socialization, regardless of the police agency or type of jurisdiction, is the Field Training Officer. It is the FTO who trains the rookie in how to do police work. While the Academy is a school program that gives the recruit the legal knowledge, it is the FTO who gives the recruit the real content knowledge, the practical training in how to be a police officer.

The trainee quickly learns that positive evaluations are achieved by performing tasks in the exact manner that the FTO performs them. The demeanor, body language, tone, attitude, and verbal behavior used by the FTO in, for instance, car stops, domestic disturbances, report calls, "pat downs," warrant checks, and arrests will be internalized by the trainee. The modeled behaviors and attitudes become the trainee's own behaviors and attitudes, and become the conditioned responses the trainee will likely use throughout his or her career. This is done because the officer's survival in tactical encounters will depend upon reacting instinctively, without delay from thoughts or decisions at the moment of impact. It is precisely the early training and development of conditioned responses recruits gain in field training that form the basis for later, reflex reactions to save their lives or the lives of the innocent.

The trainee's behavior and demeanor are observed by the FTO and communicated to other veteran officers and create the reputation or "jacket" that the new officer will wear for many years. However, the job of the Field Training Program trainers is not to teach young police officers how to maintain their concentration and presence of mind when they encouter something they were not mentally prepared for. Their job is to ensure officer safety, teach procedures involved with patrol, arrest, report writing, driving, using the radio, locating addresses, department policy and priorities, and command presence.

Command presence is critical to an officer's ability to control the incident and thus to ensure that the good people survive. The FTO makes it crystal clear to the new officer that command and control of situations and the very essence of police work require that the new officer show no emotional reaction to what he or she encounters. Any shows of emotion will cause the officer to lose control. Therefore, a major task of field training, although not included in field training guides or manuals, is to create the ability to repress conscious awareness and disclosure of distressed emotions by new police officers.

It is clear that the requirements of field training—both formal and informal—have been very successful in developing professional and safe police officers. It is also clear that the above requirements must not be changed, for the very survival of society as we want to know it depends upon the officer maintaining command and control of potentially escalating situations.

However, again we must posit the questions: Why do cops die on duty? Why is there so much talk about police divorces and family problems? Why do so many officers suffer chronic pain and physical discomfort and die younger than those whose lives they save? How can officers' physical and psychological well-being be ensured? How can cops heal from injuries that have neither entry nor exit wounds, which last for years, and for which they have no tactical training?

Actuarial forecasts for police officers show that police officers have a shorter life expectancy than the civilians whose lives they protect and save.[1] Not only is this statistic unacceptable, it is preventable. Tactics are now known that can reverse the harmful effects of police stress, as well as add to the quality and duration of cops' lives. These tactics must become a part of the training and socialization process used in police work, because these psychological survival tactics also are necessary for the safety of officers themselves.

The tragic irony is that it is simple for police officers to cope with and command emotions, physical reactions, and mental activity if they possess the tools and knowledge of why these reactions are occurring, and condition and train themselves for victory. A police officer does not have distressing emotions because he or she has "gone nuts" or weak. An officer has distressing emotions because he or she has experienced a logical reaction to a circumstance encountered. Whether the cop's "jacket" is of the toughest officer or the smallest, frailest cop in the department, distressing and/or disturbing psychological and physical reactions can and do occur, and police officers must be prepared for them.

---

1. See, for example, Violanti *et al.*, 1986, and Blum, 1999.

2: Why Cops Die:
Contributions or Compromise to Officer Safety

The most important goals of training police officers in the use of proper tactics are the successful mission to protect and serve and the prevention of assault against officers and other innocent people. Dating from the Chinese philosopher Sun Tzu's classic *The Art of War*, the guiding purpose of the study and practice of tactics has been to gain and maintain a position of advantage and control prior to and during a tactical encounter.

It is within the *application* of tactics, however, that the end result will be determined: who wins and who is vanquished, who lives and who dies, whether the good people are protected and whether the police officers will go home at the end of their watch. As Sergeant Ed Deuel of the Huntington Beach, CA Police Department says:

> We often compromise our own safety to make the case. We don't want to be criticized in court or embarrassed by a weak report, so we give the suspect freedom to act so that we can justifiably react or justifiably search. In reality, we knew this person was dangerous from the moment we saw him, but we can't just draw our weapon and search people and their cars without probable cause. So we act cool and stupid and we

don't call for backup when we should. We will look weak in front of our peers if we constantly call for backup. Yet, aggressive police officers are constantly hunting parolees. If I call for a backup too often I will get a nickname. If I don't call for backup when I should, I end up calling myself lucky.[1]

Approximately twenty-five years ago, a young police officer, Rich Wemmer, was assigned as an Academy instructor to teach tactics for the Los Angeles Police Department. He found that recruit officers were, generally, easy to deal with because they were a "blank slate." It was during in-service training that his task became more difficult, because he found that officers had developed experience in the field. Officers' field experience had formed **habits** in how they performed their work that were difficult to alter or break, because those patterns of response had been successful. Nothing bad had happened, so officers approached different circumstances the same way.

At this time, a group of instructors talked about the challenges of in-service training and the frustration they all experienced with the murders and deaths of police officers: "Why can't we look at a range of incidents?" they asked. "What was done well, what could be done better, what the suspect did that put officers in danger." The instructors studied the murders of California police officers and interviewed officers who had survived officer-involved shootings. Their beliefs were corroborated by the facts discovered during their investigation of these incidents: the great majority of incidents that an officer encountered were survivable and winnable—in other words, the officer controlled his or her own destiny.[2]

The instructors found that the use of proper tactics required, among other things, the ability to make tactical decisions. It was in *the making of decisions during conditions of threat* and *what the officer did to control subject/suspect encounters* that the safety and survivability of police officers was achieved or lost.[3]

Experts in the field of police tactics and officer safety have developed a tremendous amount of information regarding successful assaults against police officers. They have continually seen the need to train officers' minds to make tactical decisions from this body of knowledge. They know that in the best of circumstances officers have options, that their minds see a vision of tactical options from which the officer selects the solution most likely to increase the likelihood of success and survival.

The experts have studied suspect behaviors prior to and during assaults against police officers. They know that "reading the scene" is a critical task for the officer: to watch what is unusual about a person's actions; to ascertain what the suspect's reactions to the officer's presence are. Are they compliant? Is there danger? Has this individual committed a crime? What does the officer have to contend with? How can the officer act to increase safety?

These experts have felt concern that officers appear to have the tendency to rush in, walk forward, and approach the suspect—to make something happen. They have found that there are many incidents in which a suspect has deceived the officer, and that by rushing in the officer has not used all the resources that could have been applied to this circumstance.[4]

In a study of California law enforcement officers killed and assaulted in the line of duty between 1990 and 1994—performed to establish "an information base from which training curricula, policies, and procedures [could] be developed or enhanced to curtail the injury or death of California police officers"[5]—it was discovered that thirty-one police officers were feloniously murdered in the course of their duties. Each of these incidents was studied, and peers, supervisors, and co-workers of the murdered officers were interviewed. In these cases, a number of errors in officer safety were reported as the

> probable attitude or mindset of the victim peace officers just before they were murdered: The officer was overconfident; the officer was too aggressive; an attitude of carelessness or

complacency was reported; a lack of alertness or disregard for danger signs was reported; the officer maintained poor positioning; the officer relaxed too soon; a poor search technique was used; the officer was hesitant to use appropriate force; poor use of cover was reported; and the officer used improper or no use of handcuffs.[6]

In an additional study of the felonious murders of police officers, an unintended set of "behavioral descriptors" was discovered in each of fifty-four cases studied. The study reported:

It was only after several interviews with victim officers' peers and supervisors that it became apparent that similar behavioral descriptors were commonly used to describe these victim officers.... *Each of the 54 victim officers possessed several of these behavioral characteristics....* (emphasis added)

The consistently occurring characteristics of feloniously murdered victim officers were as follows. These officers were friendly to everyone and well liked by the community and department. They tended to use less force than other officers felt they would use in similar circumstances. They were hard-working and generally saw themselves as more service-oriented than other law enforcement personnel. They used force only as a last resort (peers claimed they would use force at an earlier point in similar circumstances). They didn't follow all the rules, especially in regard to arrest, confrontation with prisoners, traffic stops, and did not wait for backup (when available). The victim officers felt they could "read" others and situations and dropped their guard as a result. They tended to look for "good" in others and were characterized as "laid back" and "easygoing."[7]

The conclusion one can draw from both the above studies is that police officers' *decision-making, judgment, and the response tendencies controlled by officers' own personality have compromised officers' ability to control the scene—and resulted in the death of an officer.* These studies document the need for training and practice that is normally underemphasized in Academy and field training. Examples of such training needs are tools to maintain officers' concentration, vigilance, and accurate perceptions and judgment during threatening, unpredicted, or chaotic circumstances. In addition, officers need to be trained in techniques to engage in actions required by the elements they encounter at a scene, not their previously used personal "style" or personality.

Implications for Police Training in Tactics
There is an underlying purpose in efforts to teach tactical skills to police officers. The need for the maximal performance of the procedure or skill is an unstated expectation in all police training efforts, so the officer gains mastery in the actual field encounter being trained for. In other words, skills are taught so the officer will be capable of recognizing, assessing, and controlling scenes that contain rapidly changing, chaotic, or unpredictable events in the most proficient manner.

Control of such difficult scenes involves a simple, yet critical task to be performed by the officer. He or she must gain and maintain the initiative-control in any subject encounter in order to achieve mastery, or the subject will seize the initiative to which the officer must now react. **Initiative-control** is the term used to describe the act of taking command and control over the subject as rapidly as is possible and proper. Initiative-control counteracts the disadvantage of the fact that police officers invariably begin their attempts to control a scene somewhat behind the subject or suspect's actions.

Initiative-control is distinguished from the type of circumstance where the officer thinks to him- or herself, "Oh Shit! I didn't expect this." **Reactive-control** refers to officers' attempts to set order when they were not mentally or physically prepared for the encounter or when events appeared to be "getting away from them."

A number of reasons exist why officers may not be mentally prepared for the circumstances they encounter in the field. First, many officers have prejudged the characteristics of the contact based solely upon past experiences they have had with similar events, and not from information provided in the current scene. Second, officers may be confronted with unanticipated or rapidly changing elements that they were not apprised of earlier and did not have a readily prepared tactical plan to deal with the new circumstance that was encountered.

The development of a habit pattern of rapid and decisive action by officers is, therefore, required to gain initiative-control. Initiative-control must include a sense of the urgency of time as a critical part of tactical training, so that no delay from expectations, indecision, hesitancy, or concerns places the officer further behind the subject's actions. The consequence of the officer's falling behind the actions of the subject will be the need for officers to use greater levels of force than would have been required had the officer's response been rapid and decisive.

When the threat directed at an officer requires that he or she engage in an extremely rapid response for survival, the officer does not take the time to think consciously about the situation she or he is in. The "conscious" part of the officer's brain shuts down during survival mode. The nervous signals and brain activity that enable the officer to react for self-preservation travel and follow a much quicker reflex arc via the spinal cord (e.g., muscle reflexes). Automatic, reflex activity is an essential part of all types of police work since reaction time is an important variable in officer tactical responses.

However, reaction time in many cases also involves subconscious decision-making in which the officer performs some assessment or judgment. In these cases, reaction time includes both **assessment time** and **decision time**. Both the assessment time and, particularly, the decision time improve through the regular application of training for skill in two fundamentally important but simple mental activities:

concentration and **focusing of attention** upon the important elements in a scene that the officer encounters.

The impact upon an officer of unexpected, rapidly changing, or chaotic circumstances will often be a disruption, disturbance, or lag in time in decision-making and tactical responses until he or she accurately identifies what has to be done. This disruption occurs because the brain experiences a temporary perceptual shock when something serious happens that it wasn't ready for.

Initiative-control requires that the officer achieve mastery of the encounter by engaging in maximal performance under conditions of ambiguous, inconsistent, and/or confusing information and activity. Initiative-control requires that the officer rapidly and accurately perceives the tactical requirements of the scene and engages in decisive action to overcome the inertia brought about by the subject's actions. The officer must react to information gained from the subject's reactions to the officer's presence in order to make effective decisions regarding the levels of control that will be required to achieve mastery and control.

Some of the more recent research findings involving the training of individuals to make decisions under conditions of stress or urgency provide important lessons for tactical instructors in their efforts to develop maximal performance in police officers.[8]

It is relatively simple to teach an officer how to perform a task in a classroom setting. A class has a syllabus and plan where there is specific content being presented and the parameters of the task can be well defined. The students and instructor are able to predict the type of encounter that will be used for training purposes, and the type of tests the officer is subjected to in order to certify his or her skill in that area can be prepared for by using the class curriculum.

The cognitive or mental processing of information at a scene, however, will not occur with the same dynamics or predictability found in the classroom. The officer must retrieve the information presented to them at the scene. The officer must appraise the information to enable him or her to identify the most important and relevant aspects of the scene (and discard less relevant information). The officer must engage in rapid decision-making to develop the response that will provide him or her with initiative-control in the incident encounter. Thereafter, the officer must engage in decisive actions done as rapidly as possible to maintain initiative-control of the scene.

The proficiency of the officer in managing rapidly changing, chaotic, or unanticipated incidents will require that officers develop **adaptive expertise**. Adaptive expertise permits the individual to recognize changes in task priorities and conditions and the need to shift his or her tactical response.[9]

When officers are presented with the complex task of controlling potentially assaultive subjects, their attainment of maximal performance will require that they have, first, accurate expectations about what to expect from the subject's behaviors and reactions to their presence. Any expectations developed from past events or the officers' current emotional conditions present a possible danger of officers making inaccurate predictions of what they will encounter—instead of ensuring that they actively and accurately process the information they obtain at the current scene to determine their expectations.

Second, officers must have confidence in their ability to cope with the stressors they encounter. Third, officers must have the continuing opportunity to practice dealing with the stressors at the scene so that appropriate skills will be both developed and maintained over time. If any of these elements are missing, one cannot expect the officer to attain maximal performance of the tasks necessary to achieve officer safety and proper control of a scene.[10] Some aspect of the officer's tactical response will be compromised, and resistive or assaultive subjects will gain greater initiative-control within the encounter.

Adaptive expertise entails a deep comprehension of the conceptual nature of the problems the officer encounters, e.g., understanding the dynamics and differing profiles of assaultive behavior. Skills must be developed in an organized but *flexible* structure. That is, the officer must continue cognitive activity in the face of emergency conditions to enable him or her to register the level of threat encountered as well as any changes in the circumstance. As discussed elsewhere in this book, the part of the brain that is generally shut down when the officer encounters unanticipated elements is the part that registers changes in threat levels and circumstance and the need to shift tactics.

Adaptive expertise requires that officers participate in long-term, guided, and extensive practice experience. Their training must address normative, ongoing situations that will be frequently encountered in interactions with resistive or dangerous subjects. Thereafter, variability, ambiguity, and inconsistencies need to be inserted into the task to force the trainee to stretch his or her learning to a level of competence that permits them to rapidly respond to difficult or unanticipated events. The adaptive growth process occurs when the learning material presented is just beyond the trainee's level of competence. Solving the problems presented in the training then requires the trainee to "stretch" his or her ability and adapt his or her knowledge to new information and skills.

In order for officers to achieve maximal performance of the skills they are trained in, mastery training must be done alongside procedure or skill training because mastery enhances the development of situation awareness and adaptability.

A danger inherent in limiting training methods to procedure training is that the habits developed by experienced officers are used as a mental model from which the officer generates his or her expectations regarding the encounter. Mental models that apply past habits are likely to impede the officer's ability to correctly integrate the currently relevant information necessary to maintain officer safety within unusual tactical encounters. Training efforts must, therefore, provide a *conceptual model* that assists the officer in understanding both *how* and *why* things work. Accurate models improve performance of complex tasks, and, conversely, inaccurate models decrease task performance.[11]

Tactical encounters contain highly stressful conditions that have been shown to alter how officers apply the skills and concepts they have learned in training.[12] Therefore, exposing trainees to stressful conditions while they are practicing in event-based training[13] will enhance the likelihood that officers react decisively and accurately during a stressful event. Training efforts that are performed under low stress conditions will not likely be replicated by officers' actions in the field.

The introduction of *vague, conflicting, or imminent information* at rapid rates during a tactical encounter will increase officers' mental workload. Training *must* replicate these conditions so that the tasks of information retrieval, appraisal of threat conditions, and decision-making can be properly performed under real stress conditions. This will require that training inoculate officers with pre-exposure to the above elements in order to prevent overload, misperception, or inappropriate decision-making. These must be performed under a stressful, but not overwhelming, workload.

The elements encountered in the course of applying police field tactics are, of course, complex and varied, most of them beyond the scope of this book. I certainly lay no claim to being an expert (nor even an intermediate) in the knowledge of police tactics. In the past twenty years, however, I have seen quite a few casualties and have stood over the graves of twenty-three feloniously murdered law enforcement officers, have worked to assist many more officers and their families injured as a result of a felon's assault, and have tried to figure out why the events happened.

To obtain answers useful for police officers, I have studied the possible sources of compromise to officer safety and wellness from a *biopsychosocial*[14] and *clinical*[15] perspective. I do not believe that gaining and maintaining an advantage to ensure officer safety exists in a vacuum that only can be taught using one approach or principle.

Some of the things that compromise officer safety arise from how the officer adapts to or manages the body's biological reaction to alarm or threat. Some come from the officer's psychological reactions to single-episode onset (post-traumatic) and/or cumulative work and organizational stresses (how decision-making is accomplished during emergency conditions, mental activity, judgment, and emotion). And some arise from how the officer applies what he or she has learned and how he or she thinks and acts during stressful, unanticipated, unpredicted, or uncontrolled events.[16]

The Biological Response to Alarm

Unlike human beings, engines do not "know" if they're being threatened. Nor do they experience concerns about whether they will survive as an engine or not. When spark and fuel are provided to an engine and it is in sufficient mechanical condition, it functions the way it was designed to. Unlike the simple mechanics of the engine, however, the human being stays alive, in large measure, because of the activation of **survival instincts**. Survival instincts are necessary because they protect against unnatural death and prevent the extinction of the species.

When an individual is faced with a threat, the first instinct of importance is activated. This is the biological alarm response. The human being instinctively experiences biological arousal in preparation for decisive physical action. Whether or not that decisive physical action occurs is not important for our discussion. What is important is that an individual's internal physiological arousal level is "jacked up" under a variety of circumstances—as a human survival instinct. When an officer feels "antsy" anticipation when closing the distance to a suspect, experiences "butterflies" during a search of a darkened warehouse or alley, or has heightened senses prior to a high-risk entry, what is happening is that the body is instinctively preparing the individual to combat or adapt to some type of stressor.

What police officers have not understood as well is that while the individual's instinctive, preparatory biological response to a perceived threat is *generally* a process of arousal, survival instincts in individuals may also entail a type of physiological response that causes the slowing, inhibition, or complete stoppage of tactical thinking, aggressive behavior, or the amount of activity in muscles and organs of the body.[17]

When stress arousal becomes excessively intense or chronic (cumulative stress) in duration, some impairment will result. The human brain contains separate areas of activity. Each area is responsible for a task or specific group of tasks that enable the individual to respond effectively to threat. One part (the neocortex, or cerebral cortex) allows the individual to use information received by the senses. This part works to interpret the information available at the scene to determine what level of threat the individual is faced with. It then appraises the body's ability to withstand the threat and decides upon a response. (The cerebral cortex is concerned with communication, decision-making, problem-solving activities, planning, and the learning of skills.)

Any loss of concentration, assessment or analytical activity, or shutdown of conscious thinking in the officer prior to or during a tactical encounter due to the officer not being mentally prepared will disrupt or extinguish the ability to make rapid and accurate decisions. The loss of purposeful thinking during an encounter will impair the officer's ability to develop, alter, and/or implement a tactical plan based upon the principles and practices of tactics she or he has learned.

What an officer hopes and expects during a loss of concentration is that the actual circumstance he or she must now respond to goes along with the way the officer's perceptions, expectations, training, and personality predicted it would. When this "shutdown" in the cerebral cortex activity occurs, officers will react either from previously conditioned patterns of response developed during training activities, or by their own expectations and habits.

The **limbic system** serves an important role in our response to stress because of its role as the emotional control center for the human brain. The limbic system is comprised of numerous nerve structures that activate emotional responses when officers, for example, find themselves in a circumstance they were not mentally or tactically prepared for. Feelings of urgency, fear, helplessness, loss of control, anxiety, depression, and anger are generated in the structures of the limbic system.

The brain has one branch of the nervous system (sympathetic nervous system) that prepares our bodies for action. Its effect on the organs it activates is that of generalized arousal.[18] Another branch the brain uses in its reactions to threat (the parasympathetic nervous system) is concerned with quieting the body and restoring it to resting levels. Its general effects are those of slowing and maintaining a type of *status quo* to enable the body to recover from demands placed upon it. While a parasympathetic reaction that lowers the level of the body's exertion assists an individual in "cooling down" from intense exercise, it greatly endangers that same individual during the course of a fierce struggle for survival.

When presented with a threat, the brain releases "stress" hormones, some of which increase and some that lessen arousal. A hormone called **cortisol** controls or modulates the body's arousal level. Cortisol is released when the brain is engaged in the appraisal of threat. Once the level of threat is appraised, the brain assesses the body's ability to respond to that threat.

When the brain perceives the danger to be moderate or severe, cortisol acts to turn stores of energy into glucose to fuel an individual's emergency response. Where there is no grave danger perceived by the organism, or after the brain perceives that the threat has ended, cortisol inhibits the stress response and returns the brain to normal functioning. When the brain appraises the threat as so extreme as to overwhelm the individual's ability to manage it, however, cortisol attempts to protect the survival of the body by lessening and/or shutting down the body's activity or energy.

Concerning police officers' physiology, parasympathetic nervous system shutdown most often occurs in two conditions. When officers don't expect to encounter much in the way of threat, there is a tendency to relax or let down their guard. When officers are unexpectedly or suddenly presented with extreme danger and they perceive no chance or ability to escape, the body's functioning and activity and arousal may be lessened, shut down, and extinguished. When something happens that interferes with or shuts down an officer's mental concentration and accurate appraisal of threat, the likelihood that the officer will use proper tactics is lessened—as are the chances of victory and survival.

Conversely, officers may place themselves in harm's way by reacting impulsively or heedlessly because they are more "jacked" than they are careful. When the call or contact requires a "3" level of arousal intensity to control it effectively, but the officer tends to operate on a "9" level on this type of contact, the officer may rush to try to make an arrest and be ambushed by deceptive suspect actions.

Psychological Reactions to Police Work

The type of mental activity that occurs during officers' assessment, prioritizing, and decision-making does not exist in a vacuum. It is affected by a number of different variables, especially how the individual officer reacts to stressful circumstances.

An officer's first task when arriving at the scene of a call for service, a traffic stop, or encounters with suspects in the field is to make an assessment of the scene. All subsequent plans for cover, concealment, dangers, and resources to be used, etc., are based upon these initial assessments. Whether or not the officer lives or dies will, in large measure, be determined by the timeliness, accuracy, and flexibility of the officer's analytic thinking—i.e., his or her ability to accurately register the level of threat the he or she faces and the possible need to shift the tactical plan he or she had initially intended to use.

The type of thinking required for such analysis, decision-making, problem-solving, and/or tactical planning is **sequential** in nature: first A, then B, then C, then D. Officers need to assess the makeup of the scene they are encountering and what type of situation they are dealing with. They examine how the subject or suspect is reacting to their presence, whether the subjects possess weapons, what levels of danger or threat they're encountering, their concerns, possible cover, backup, and tactical plans.

"Oh, It's Going to Be One of These"

There is a logical reason why police officers begin to develop expectations about what they will encounter when they arrive at a scene. The mind of a police officer does not easily tolerate unknown circumstances without becoming tense. This is because unknown circumstances prevent the officer from using a previously developed tactical plan. He or she is, therefore, placed in a reactive mode and not psychologically prepared for what may be encountered. Police officers tend to be uncomfortable with feelings of uncertainty. Therefore, the officer's mind often begins to create a scenario of the encounter, because such a scenario serves to reduce tension in the officer. In other words, officers begin to develop expectations about the nature of a contact before that contact is actually made.

Our expectations determine what we see. If police officers expect to encounter an unimportant false alarm at a silent alarm call (perhaps the last several silent alarms were false alarms), there is a tendency for the officer to consider the situation less threatening, because such a lessening in threat has been experienced in a number of prior alarm calls. The officer's expectations that the call will not be problematic aids in temporarily decreasing uncomfortable feelings of uneasiness he or she may have. While I understand the officer may feel good at the time, I believe these expectations are extremely dangerous. Pre-existing expectations about a type of call that have been used by officers to reduce their tension have led to tragic underestimations of threats. Because of this, officers have found themselves in

47

circumstances they were not mentally, emotionally, or tactically prepared for.

The Trickery of Expectations

One officer I debriefed had been called to a day-care facility on two occasions to respond to a complaint. The estranged ex-boyfriend of the owner of the facility was alleged to have been lounging around the facility, staring at the owner with a fixed stare, and generally frightening her and other staff. The officer responded to the day-care facility and tried to contact the ex-boyfriend on two occasions. The subject reacted in a passive, meek, and withdrawing manner to the officer's presence.

In each contact with the subject, the officer felt an increasing confidence in his control of the situation. The subject did not demonstrate aggressiveness or offer any active resistance in either contact. Without his being consciously aware of it, the officer had begun to develop expectations of how the subject would react to him. These expectations developed from the good feeling of control the officer had experienced during two prior contacts with the same type of compliant, even "wimpy" subject.

There was now a third complaint made by the owner of the day-care facility regarding this subject. The same officer responded, but this time the subject—now a suspect—did not behave in the same manner he had in the two prior contacts. Standing in front of the day-care facility, the suspect's demeanor was, according to the officer, "pumped, tight, and rigid, like he could explode." The suspect began to verbally threaten the officer and advance toward him. The suspect's hand then disappeared into a jacket he was wearing—one that was different from the description previously broadcast by dispatch. He was screaming at the officer, "I'm going to kill you," and his behavior seemed highly consistent with his verbal threats.

The officer reacted with decisiveness and courage to the suspect's potentially lethal threats. The officer was married; he had loved ones he wanted to return to after his duty watch. The officer also had high moral values, and was greatly concerned after the incident (which resulted in the use of lethal force) that he had done the correct and right thing. He felt bad, and the only reason he could think of for feeling bad was that he had done something wrong. He was therefore uneasy.

The officer had experienced a type of shock reaction during this very dangerous incident. Time appeared to slow down a great deal; he didn't hear sounds around him that were actually quite loud. Without realizing it, the officer had actually made a prediction of how the suspect would react to his presence on this third encounter. His brain had associated the two previous contacts he had had with the suspect and predicted a similar suspect behavior on this one. Without being consciously aware he was doing so, this highly professional officer had developed expectations that said to him: "Oh, it's going to be one of these."

The department's trauma support team—a team made up of police officers trained in the technique of psychological debriefing—performed an initial debriefing with the officer immediately after the investigating detectives had taped an interview with him. The officer was later referred to me for a second debriefing.

During the course of this debriefing, I told the officer some relatively simple reasons why he was not feeling better after this incident. I indicated that when an officer has prior contact with some circumstance or person, he or she will naturally have a tendency to begin to use the experience on this prior contact as a "base" for what he or she will "need to do" during future encounters and how the encounters will "go" as well.

The officer came to understand that he was feeling uneasy because he had predicted what the suspect would do instead of analyzing what the suspect was doing at the present time. The officer was actually remembering past behaviors observed earlier as he was engaging with the suspect the third time. Therefore, he was shocked and surprised when things did not go the way he had expected. I suggested to him that he was logically upset because he'd been taken by surprise and had, as a result, felt momentary feelings of a loss of control; he certainly had not done "wrong" in this incident.

When an officer's brain has predicted a single, minimal degree of threat but encounters another, serious threat instead, some disruption in perception can be expected to occur. This is actually a logical physiological response to unanticipated emergency circumstances. It is not a "sign" that the officer is not in complete control of him- or herself.

Certainly the officer in the above example could have beaten himself up for not **reading the scene** properly. Because he held such high moral and professional standards for himself, the officer had mistakenly interpreted his post-incident feelings of discomfort as indicating that he had "done something wrong" and he felt badly about it. According to the investigating detectives from the county's officer team, the officer had conducted himself properly and courageously.

Indeed, several eyewitnesses each had reported the exact same actions by the suspect and the officer. Witnesses reported that the officer had, several times in a loud and clear voice, ordered the suspect to stop. "Drop your weapon," he had said. "This can be ended without anyone being hurt." As if he were entreating the suspect, he had continued: "Don't make me do this." However, the eyewitnesses reported that the suspect did not comply with the officer's commands and advanced and assaulted the officer in a manner that had frightened them and represented a threat to lives.

I provided the officer with an understanding of the causes for his perfectly logical reactions to the threat he had encountered: "When the suspect refused to allow you to save him, and at the last possible moment," I told him, "you acted in a decisive and courageous manner. You saved the woman and children that this guy was going to harm. I can understand you're not feeling thrilled, because you were surprised." The officer came to realize and accept that he had been made victim of a coward's way out of his difficulties: "Suicide by Cop."

It has long been acknowledged in the fields of law enforcement and psychology that sensory distortions occur to police officers during certain high-risk encounters. Lapses in officer concentration during an encounter with lethal threat, the appearance of a slowing of motion, muffled sounds and recoil, detail errors during post-incident reporting, and, in many cases, a lack of conscious awareness by the officer that he or she was using serious or lethal force have been reported by a majority of police officers during post-incident psychological debriefings I have performed. It has been my experience that these sensory changes are more likely to occur on patrol, because almost all patrol encounters contain some degree of unanticipated encounter. When they have encountered unanticipated events, officers have reacted based upon their training, their previous practice, and what they had experienced successfully in prior encounters. Sometimes their responses worked and sometimes they did not.

I strongly believe that sensory distortions that officers have reported experiencing during lethal encounters occur in direct reaction to **unanticipated elements** contained within the scene. In my clinical work with officers, I have observed a consistently occurring, predictable "thread" running through a great many of their reactions.

If the officer has not been surprised by the elements that he or she encounters (through the use of information provided to the officers for an incident in which the elements were known, or through their use of analysis rather than expectation), his or her reactions to the threat are not likely to contain any type of shock or distorted perception. If, however, officers encounter unanticipated elements—i.e., expecting one thing but encountering another—they have a much greater likelihood of some disturbance in their perceptions of the event, and some post-incident stress because of a shock reaction they go through.

Sgt. Ed Deuel and I decided to conduct an experiment in training methods with the Huntington Beach, California Police Department Training Division, 1997–1999. We believed that if officers were presented with ambush or surprise circumstances during in-service training simulations, using experienced officers over a period of time—and with repetitions of the scenario performed until such time that the officer consistently prevailed over the adversary—then it would be less likely that he or she would be shocked, experience any sensory distortions, or hesitate (or freeze) in responding to the threat. We believed this to be true because the officer's brain would now be conditioned to respond effectively to unanticipated circumstances and thus the officer would be more likely to control and overcome the threat.

Sgt. Deuel himself told me of his own surprise when he unexpectedly came upon an armed robbery in progress while on duty as a "brand-new sergeant." On that night, his thoughts and expectations were not on tactical readiness; he took for granted that his work was tactically excellent. However, Deuel's skill as an officer— and his body armor, which took two bullets from a Tec-9 in his chest—saved him by allowing him to take immediate, decisive action and extinguish the threat. He was, however, surprised when, in a video re-enactment of his shooting,[19] the actor playing the suspect turned toward him. "Wait a second," said Deuel, "you're supposed to be moving extremely slowly...the suspect moved and turned in an extreme slow motion...." This was not true. It just appeared to Deuel that way. During the surprise encounter, Deuel also heard no sounds during the battle.

As discussed, range training, while greatly beneficial to police officers in allowing them to master the use of their equipment, cannot be expected to prepare officers completely for actual encounters with lethal threat in the field—threats that most often involve multiple suspects moving around and possible officers and/or citizens in the line of danger. How valuable the training of police officers is specifically for unanticipated circumstances in their encounters was shown clearly in an incident in the same police department.

Throughout their careers, officers respond to many interrupted or hang-up "911" calls. Time after time, officers find a relatively simple explanation for the call and the hang-up. Without being aware of it, officers can easily develop a laid-back attitude when a "911 hang-up" is broadcast. It's not surprising to hear the first officer on the scene cancel a backup and communicate "Code 4" or "Everything is hunky-dory" prior to a careful search of the premises. Indeed, officers who call for backup too often get a reputation as wimps who can't patrol their beat on their own.

Heroic Acts

One day, however, a police officer on Day Watch answered a call from a beauty salon. Three women customers were in the salon and one of them had her small child in tow. A dangerous felon had entered the salon and demanded both flesh and money from the adult women and child. He locked the women and the child in a small storage room and made it clear he was going to rape them.

One of the employees of the salon quietly picked up the telephone so the suspect would not know a "911" call was being made. The employee dialed the emergency number and then put down the phone without speaking into it, since any conversation would have alerted the suspect.

The police officer who took the call was a senior officer in the department, a veteran of over twenty years of police work. He was the officer whom the new officers in the department looked up to and wanted to emulate. He responded to the address provided him in the broadcast of a "911 hang-up," never really expecting to face imminent death and a fight for his life. After all, in numerous other occasions there had been some relatively simple explanation for the call and the hang-up.

From the salon, the suspect observed the officer's approach and could have escaped through a rear door located next to the storage room and never been seen again. However, the suspect decided to remain in the store, kill the cop, and then go back for the women. Posing as an employee by putting on a hair-cutter's apron, the suspect walked out and greeted the officer, carrying a bag that contained a gun. Without warning, at a distance of from six to ten feet, he opened fire at the officer.

Although the officer simultaneously received three bullets to his left arm and two bullets to the upper torso (which were stopped by his second chance vest), he managed to unsnap his weapon, draw it, and take a position face-to-face with the suspect. The officer returned fire, striking the suspect ten times. The suspect went down. It was only when he couldn't operate his hand-set radio that the officer realized he couldn't move his left arm. He realized he was bleeding heavily and retreated to the front door area where he asked citizens to help him. He used his portable radio to call for help.

The officer later stated that this incident occurred exactly like the training scenarios he had recently been exposed to. He'd been unexpectedly ambushed in one of the training scenarios and had been successful in his ability to draw and return fire in a life-and-death situation where the suspect was less than ten feet away and the officer's weapon had been holstered and snapped.

There was no decision-making performed in this incident. When the officer was faced with this grave threat, he acted with a spontaneous, aggressive, life-saving, and successful sequence of actions. The officer had practiced this behavior enough that a habit had developed in his brain. Therefore, when he was ambushed, he reacted in a decisive and successful manner. The officer was not slowed by any shock or indecision; he didn't hesitate or freeze. He didn't need to take the time to make decisions about what to do. He was prepared and ready to do it.

A few days later, as the officer was lying in his hospital bed with his wounded, broken arm and bruised chest, the husband of one of the women in the salon came to visit him with his wife and child. Sobbing, he thanked this heroic officer for saving his family.

Development of Habit

The brain will not do what an officer hopes or expects it to do. It will do as it has practiced. Repeated patterns or sequences of behavior that an officer performs will change the pathways through which neural activity occurs in the brain. When an officer suddenly encounters a grave, unanticipated, and immediate threat, it is unlikely that he or she will have the luxury of time to make decisions about what to do. His or her brain will follow previously conditioned mental and behavioral patterns.

Either through repeated experiences or one severe or intense experience, the structure and direction of nerves in the brain can change. If, for example, officers have succeeded in calming and defusing several potentially escalating encounters by talking to the subjects in a respectful and reasonable manner, then, over the course of time and repetitions of these successful verbal contacts, they are likely to become habituated or conditioned to using these tools. Then, when they encounter grave, unanticipated, and immediate threats, they may be predisposed to continue to "...try to talk and give verbal direction to a suspect who was trying to murder them."[20]

Such habit behaviors are automatically (unconsciously) performed. It's not that the officer is thinking about doing it; it is that he or she is *very likely to do it* whenever the source of the habit (such as the successful use of verbal tactics above) is encountered. Put in other terms, unless you concentrate upon assessing *this here-and-now scene* with *this subject* under *these conditions*, you are likely to do what is familiar to you when you are in unfamiliar territory. These unconsciously performed patterns by police officers are sometimes, in the aftermath of an officer's injury or death, referred to in a critical manner as **complacency**.

There is a plaque in the sergeant's office in the Orange County, California Sheriff's Academy. It lists "20 Fatal Mistakes" made by police officers.[21] Many of these mistakes involve some type of compromise or lapse in officers' mental activity, the accuracy of their perceptions, or how they exercised judgment. It may be tiredness, relaxing too soon, overconfidence, false bravado, lack of self-control, or discipline.

Is it just fatigue that makes officers complacent? Is it a question of underestimating the current threat and relaxing too soon simply because the officer has now spent several moments with a suspect (a person normally becomes more relaxed with another with the passing of time)? Is it overconfidence in a particular type of approach or tactic that restricts what resources the officer can use against the threat? Is it "tombstone courage" that causes an officer to rush to contact with a suspect in order to make something happen? Or is it a lack of self-control of the body's arousal level and/or lack of self-discipline in the choices of action the officer takes? Whatever the specific cause, it is highly likely that what occurred to the officer in his or her tragic error in tactics was a result of uncontrolled and unconscious use of habits that have "worked" for the officer in the past.

Because threats come at officers in many, many ways—most of which cannot be predicted prior to the immediate contact with the threat—a primary task communicated by several expert law enforcement trainers and tactical instructors is to combat complacency in police officers. Within the general term "complacency" one can observe a number of possible errors made by officers during tactical encounters.[22]

It doesn't matter whether an officer is the most experienced tactical instructor or expert on the department. When an officer's thinking is preoccupied or distracted by frustrations, irritability, emotional distress or depression, worry, or anticipation of some event, the part of his or her brain that creates emotion starts firing. When that happens, the part of the brain that registers threat and the need to shift tactics—the cerebral cortex—loses two-thirds of its spark, fuel, and activity.

If officers approaching a subject are concerned about making the individual happy about police contact, the officers' brains may underestimate or ignore signals that tell them they are placing themselves in a position of disadvantage or danger. As one supervising tactical instructor advised:

> You can be polite...the subject has to be aware that the officer they face is in command...you do that with command presence. What was going through the officer's mind...am I going to be held liable? You deal with the parolee and you deal with the victim. You can smoothe someone's feathers later...the parolee will read a polite officer as, "he's doable...."[23]

Another supervising tactical instructor suggests that officers need to be trained to avoid getting "sucked in by the situation." A domestic dispute, an "assist the person" call with a mentally disturbed individual, an "unknown trouble" call where the description of the scene is minimal or conflictual, a woman screaming that she needs help—all these have the potential to cause officers to lose their **presence of mind** as they engage the encounter.[24]

Presence of Mind
Presence of mind refers to a critically important act of concentrating upon a task, a conscious analysis of imminent threat, and a conscious choice of tactic and force options—all in the presence of an emergency. Tactical instructors often refer to presence of mind in the face of an emergency as "decision-making under pressure."

Presence of mind also refers to an honest self-evaluation: "To thine own self be true." Officers need to ask themselves whether they tend to rush in a little bit or need to engage banteringly with people. An officer who is prepared, ready, and able is one who will think about the what-if's, but not lock on to preconceived notions. Uncontrolled emotional activity and/or uncontrolled habit tendencies disrupt the type of thinking required for presence of mind.

Every police officer worth his or her salt has encountered an incident significant or profound enough to maintain its impact upon how the officer felt, acted, or performed his or her work, even after the call was cleared. Then, when some subsequent encounter contains similar elements to the one that so impacted the officer, the officer may experience the very same reactions and act as if the very same reactions were what were called for in the current incident.

In the aftermath of traumatic incident encounters, many officers have found that they changed the way they worked. In one national sample of police officers participating in research on stress in police work,[25] sixty percent reported that the immediate and long-term impact of disturbing incidents had changed the way they worked. Some reported engaging in more officer-initiated activity, others less. Others reported greater or less fear experienced in subsequent contact.

Regardless of the manner in which post-incident reactions have impacted an officer, however, the officer's ability to maintain effective presence of mind and situation-appropriate action is likely to be impaired. The lasting impact of a past event can influence or alter an officer's current response to a threat.

Police officers today are often more concerned with what others or society might say about their work than before. I have debriefed and evaluated hundreds of officers' uses of force in the last twenty years, yet I have found in the past eight years (since the 1992 incident involving Rodney King), and with increasingly greater frequency of occurrence, that even though the officers' use of force later turned out to be justified, they had allowed the suspect the ability to threaten them to a point where greater levels of force were required. Officers seem hesitant to contain and command a situation assertively and aggressively for fear of being criticized, punished, or sued. More and more media attention has been placed upon both civil and criminal legal action taken against officers in the course of their work.

Inadequate physical and mental conditioning has resulted in the deaths of police officers. Officers' safety depends upon their effective use of decision-making and rapid, decisive response to threats. And yet, a major impediment to officers' ability to maintain effective decision-making or presence of mind during emergency lies in their extreme reluctance to appear as if they have "messed up." Because officers are constantly second-guessed for their actions and decisions in every encounter in which they engage, over time a defensive, self-protective mask is formed that covers over officers' potentially fatal insecurities, self-doubts, or errors in judgment.

No one is suggesting that police officers become mean, grumpy, or treat everyone like a criminal. However, another of my "rules of life" is pertinent here: You never know what precaution saved you, so it is stupid not to use each and every one of them, no matter what you do. You never know what mistake killed you, so make sure you never make the same one twice.

Like many of us, I hate making mistakes. What I do is embrace them, instead. I don't ignore them. I don't ever want them to occur again. Officer safety would be well served with some alteration in the standard method law enforcement employs in stressful circumstances: "If no one saw it, and I don't think about it, it doesn't bother me. If it doesn't bother me, I have no problem with it. If I have no problem with it, I'm *okfine*."

Isn't this approach to stress in some way a surrender? We need to develop a habit of overcoming adversity and countermanding any and all threat to a successful outcome by confronting and managing the situation, not cloaking or "stuffing away" the areas in which we are less strong.

---

1. Personal communications, 1999.
2. Wemmer, 1999.
3. Wemmer, Osuna, Deuel, Miller, Bardzik, 1999. Heal 2000.
4. Wemmer, 1999.
5. LEOKA Study, California Commission on Police Officer Standards and Training, 1996.
6. Ibid., pp. 1–17.
7. Federal Bureau of Investigation, U.S. Department of Justice, *Killed in the Line of Duty: A Study of Selected Felonious Killings of Law Enforcement Officers*, 1992. p. 32
8. See, for example, Cannon-Bowers & Salas, 1998; Kozlowski, 1998.
9. Kozlowski, 1998.
10. Cannon-Bowers & Salas, 1998.
11. Ibid.

12. Blum, 1994.
13. Cannon-Bowers & Salas, 1998.
14. Everly, 1986; *et al.*
15. Blum, 1994; 1998.
16. The reader interested in the study of tactics will find much material to study. An excellent and easy-to-read example is Heal, 2000.
17. Engel, 1971; Gellhorn, 1968; Selye, 1981; Gray, 1985; *et al.*
18. Everly, 1989.
19. Wemmer, 1986.
20. California Law Enforcement Officers Killed and Assaulted in the Line of Duty, 1990–1994 Report, 1996, pp. 1–48. In beat patrol, for example, an officer will likely develop his or her own "style" of working his or her area of responsibility. Officers develop routines and usually predictable patterns. They develop habits. (See Bardzik, personal communications, 1999.)
21. Bardzik, 1999.
22. It is not solely on-duty habit patterns that can create complacency or error in an officer's response to threat. It can happen if an officer is preoccupied by circumstances in his or her personal life, in actions of the police organization, in actions of city councils or town government that troubles him or her in the ability to engage in the analytic thinking that is required for proper tactics.
23. Bardzik, 1999.
24. Miller, 1999.
25. Blum, 1998.

3: "I've Been Shot!"
Maintaining the Will to Survive

I n the aftermath of the murder of police officers, law enforcement has undertaken investigations and studies to identify the causal factors responsible for these tragic losses. The results of these investigations have identified such critically important factors as use of a tactical plan, avoiding isolated action, using effective communication, using proper tactics, familiarity with equipment, maintaining a strong physical condition, and possessing a positive mental attitude.

In far too many cases, I have reviewed studies about the murder of an officer in which the loss of her or his will to survive or, as it is termed, "positive mental attitude," was identified as the probable causal factor.[1] In these cases, an officer has surrendered his or her life because he or she experienced a psychology of defeat. In other words, the officer's assessment was: "This is too much for me."

Studies have been performed of incidents in which a police officer was assaulted by a lethal threat. Tactics have been developed from these studies and are taught to thousands of police applicants in the Academy and in in-service advanced officer training courses. Videotape and written re-enactments are made of shootings that have involved officers, deputies, agents, or investigators. Collectively, these studies and tactics are designed to permit officers to gain the initiative, maintain control of the encounter, and succeed in their objectives during on-duty encounters. A major goal of the use of police tactics is to prevent the officer from being successfully attacked.

Officer survival requires, however, something in addition to the use of proper tactics. When an officer has been shot, stabbed, or hit, that officer needs to maintain the will, drive, commitment, demand, and certainty of a simple truth: "I will not be defeated. I will not die. I am not done yet. I have more to do. I have family to see again. I will not let this circumstance defeat me. I will not surrender. I will not die."

This, one would think, would be obvious. Yet, police officers have died with no vital organ involved in their wound or injury. So we need to ask ourselves why officers sometimes give up. What does it really mean to "lose the will to survive" or "lose the winning attitude"? What compromises the will to survive in police officers? Is the will to survive something some people don't have?

In the course of debriefing scores of assaulted police over twenty years, I have found that many young officers were amazed that the assault occurred in the first place. They were struck by the shock of actually being "gotten to" by felons. After all, they thought, they had been trained in preventing assault. Yet they had received no training in what to do after an assault upon them was successful.

A Hero's Will

The crook was called the "John Wayne Bandit." He had hit many of the major restaurants in the city. He had been given his name because, each time he'd struck, he'd gotten bolder and more aggressive. It had reached the point where he'd kick the doors, "cap some rounds" into the ceiling to scare patrons, pistol-whip the manager, and generally terrorize people. However, by the time officers had responded to the call, the crook was gone. This had been going on for two and a half years.

An analysis of where and when the crook had struck suggested there would be another hit soon, although patrol officers were told not to engage the crook directly at the scene but go to a close by residential area. Restaurant managers were provided with alarms controlled by a remote button held by the manager. Pushing the remote button superseded all normal radio transmissions, reported "armed robbery in progress," and gave the name and location of the restaurant.

There was an officer doing an overtime shift, trading duty watches as a favor to a friend. He was twenty-seven years old and had ten months on the job. His excellent police work had resulted in his getting a good reputation in a very short period of time. Others in patrol gave him the name "shit magnet" because things happened whenever he would make a stop. If he asked for a backup, other officers knew there was a felony involved. "After a while," the officer told me, "everyone in the city would roll when I requested backup, because they knew something 'good' was going to happen."

The officer had a report pending from the day before, when he had arrested two burglars leaving a condominium complex. It was a drizzly, cold night and he was cruising a residential area. "I wasn't intending to do anything that would give me any extra work," he told me. "I had this report holding and it was overtime. I had just requested permission to come into the station, finish the report, and end the shift. I received permission to come in and finish up. All of a sudden the emergency channel reports a "211" (armed robbery) in progress at _____ restaurant. I went, 'Oops, it's right across the street.'

"I responded to a residential tract behind the restaurant," he continued, "remembering what the detectives had told us. I was anxious....I wanted to catch this guy. Having the rep of 'shit magnet' was a burden. If you get involved in something good it's an adrenaline rush itself...plus [there's] the satisfaction of other officers saying, 'Way to go!' "

The officer hit his "kill" switch, extinguishing all lighting in or on his patrol vehicle. He began to cruise slowly. As he turned southbound, he saw someone walking to a car. "That's him," the officer said. "Not a 'possible.' That's him. In my mind there was no question." The suspect entered a vehicle and, slowly, at about 25 mph, headed southbound. His vehicle was driving without any lights.

"We're both going southbound. I don't think he's seen me yet. But we go under a streetlight and I think it illuminated me. The suspect's lights go on and he speeds up. He doesn't stop for the stop sign. I put out 'possible suspect fleeing' and give my location. I'm thinking, 'The race is on. This is where it gets to be fun. We're going to have a good pursuit. And nobody gets away from me.'

"You have to appreciate the fact that, at ten months, you're doing so well you get that sense of invulnerability. And you get that big 'S' [Superman sign] on your chest like 'Everyone is going to submit to me or lose to me.' That is the kind of feeling I had.

"I got on the gas...put my lights on. The suspect turned right at the corner and I made a right-hand turn to follow him. I was surprised by the suspect...the suspect had stopped...he was waiting for me.

"Then he took off again, slowly. I went, 'Whoa! What is it with this guy? He's not playing by the rules. He's supposed to run, and I'm supposed to chase him and get the cavalry on him and then we all chase him.' I know that something is wrong...that this is not normal...we're going really slow."

The officer began to assess the local streets and possible avenues of escape the suspect might choose. He still had the mindset, as he said, "He's waiting to make his move to get away."

The officer put out his information and location again, and cited the suspect's license plate. He hoped that his transmissions would bring the "cavalry." "I'm confused because I look at my rearview mirror and there's nobody there. I wasn't getting any response back. This confused me. When you're the shit magnet and everyone's coming at every one of your stops and all of a sudden nobody's there....Why? I thought I was doing everything right."

The suspect again changed his behavior. "All of a sudden he's on the gas. He makes a right turn and, it's like, 'OK, now the chase is on.'"

"Well, I make my right turn at a high rate of speed and as I come around the corner he had stopped. He sucked me in, big time. Man, that's not the way the game is played. I get this big, 'Oh shit' feeling. I know at that point it's going to be a shooting. I even visualize myself in the shooting before it happens.

"I knew that I was going to be shot. 'I better prepare, I've got to do something.' It was fear. After feeling the fear then I stepped into another stage: 'I'd better prepare myself.'"

The officer reached down, unsnapped his holster, and said, "OK. Here's what I want to do. I want to get my gun, have my door open, and move into a position of defense behind the door and at the frame of the car in the 'V.'"

The imminent combat now created some alteration in the officer's senses: "Everything was so slow...I thought I had lots of time for thinking this....In a very short time that's what I did. I told myself all the things I wanted to do."

At that moment in the situation, the officer suddenly shifted his focus and recognized the need to contact dispatch again: "This is going to be my last transmission before it happens. I tell dispatch my location...what I'm doing...I still get no response. He sees me on the radio. His car comes to a complete stop...no brake lights....He either put it in park or...the emergency brake....His door comes flying open."

While the officer was engaged in analysis, planning, and concentration, without being aware he was doing so, he was moving to a position of defense: "Other than pre-programming myself, I have no idea how I got to that position. I can remember being at the car door with a gun in my hand and returning fire.

"He's coming at me. I see flashes coming out of the muzzle of his gun. They're pretty significant flashes, not just a little pop. They're thundering in my vision like, 'BOOOMMM BOOOOMMMM,' but I hear nothing. As he's running towards me, the first two rounds are supposed to have hit me in the upper chest. They came right over the steering wheel and lodged in the seat—but I wasn't there. That's how fast I moved. But one of them did catch me in my right arm. The upper bicep.

"I'm returning fire. I didn't feel the one that hit me. Another round splintered and hit me in the head. I didn't feel that one either. The suspect comes running at me. I'm feeling ineffective. I'm throwing rounds out and nothing is stopping him." (Although the officer was unaware of it at the time, one of his first two rounds had hit the suspect in the area of the chest and torso.)

"He's still coming. Again, that's not how it's supposed to work. He's supposed to be falling and he's not doing it. He comes up and sticks his gun in my car window and shove[s] the gun at my upper torso and caps off a round. He hits me in my left shoulder and I start to move to my right with the impact, across the seat.

"I see him hit me. I can see him move the gun to my lower torso because he wants to put one in my body. What he winds up doing is hitting my elbow...shatters it...immediately excruciating pain. My hand hits the seat and my gun goes flying under the floorboard. It's another 'Oh shit' feeling. This hurts like a sonofabitch. It doesn't make me less aggressive but it makes me aware of the disadvantage I'm in.

"I see him roll and then come up at the rear of my trunk. I can see him standing with one hand on the trunk...his gun pointed at my car. It was a great tactical position for him and I was thinking, 'OK, I'm really feeling hurt.' I could feel blood coming down my face. I'm lying there and I'm thinking, 'Do I go for my gun and hope that I'm quick enough to get my gun and try to defend myself, because he's going to come up for another attack if I do that? If I go for my gun he's going to immediately rush up from his defensive position and come in and it's going to be a gun battle in my car.'

"And then I think, 'There's got to be enough blood on me to where he may think I'm dead. Do I play possum?' I make the decision. I remember from the Academy saying, 'Here is where they get you.' I just weighed my options. To try to get my gun was not the smartest thing to do. I was badly hurt, and I might not even be able to get it. It was a tactical decision.

"I'm waiting for the shot. I know it's going to hurt. I'm telling myself, 'If he shoots me I will survive. I will. He may shoot me again, but it won't be fatal.' You have to have a mental will...to program yourself to know that things will be OK. I'm calling upon my instincts to want to survive and win no matter what."

This was a totally new experience to the officer. I asked him what he called upon, what experience base or mental process had been done to permit him to maintain such a powerful will to survive. He thought for a moment. "You know where cops have dreams? Where they can't hit the suspect? I had dreams like that before. I would be running around a corner chasing a suspect, and there he would be when I turned the corner...waiting for me...stabbing me....I'd wake up scared," he recalled. "I would go, 'OK, we're going back...to sleep...we're pickin' it up....' I would go to sleep thinking, 'OK, we're going to win.' I wouldn't go to sleep until I told myself, 'Here's the outcome....This is where we win.' "

I told the officer that the mental processes he had instinctively performed in the night were a perfect example of pre-programming himself for success. He said that he had not known he was doing that, but told me he felt that's exactly what he *was* doing. "I would do that every time I had a bad dream. That's all I can recall that made me draw from that."

The officer then felt the car door open and come off his foot (he was lying across his seat with one leg hanging out of the door with the door against his foot). "I knew he was there. I was anticipating the shot. But the next thing I know, my car is moving and when my car starts moving I know that he's back in his car and he's gone, because that's the only way my car could start rolling (his vehicle had been front bumper to rear bumper against the suspect's vehicle).

The officer was severely wounded. "I can remember lying there for a couple of seconds thinking, 'You know, I don't have time to die. I've got too many things…I've got kids to raise.' I saw my kids and saw I had to survive. I had to do something.

"And then I remember Bob Smithson [L.A.P.D., Retired, a nationally known expert on officer survival], my officer survival instructor in the Academy…and this man has some tremendous command presence. I remember him standing in front of us, face-to-face close, saying, 'The only cop who dies is the one that wants to die. If you want to live you will live.' And then he told us about certain cops that died with non-vital wounds. It was like he was standing in my car and he said this."

With that recollection of his survival instructor, the officer felt as if someone had slapped him. He grabbed the steering wheel with his right hand. He pulled himself up. He sat up in the car. When he sat up he could see the suspect four or five houses away from him going westbound up the street. He looked down, turned on his overhead lights, and went in pursuit of the suspect. The officer put out his call number over the radio, that he'd been shot, and where the suspect was heading.

"What I found out later…a major frustration for me was that nothing was getting responded to. It turns out there was bad transmission that night, and the manager kept pressing the alarm that would supersede the normal green channel frequencies and, while he was pressing, my transmissions were being covered. One of the other officers had gone directly to the restaurant and was told to follow a different suspect vehicle in the opposite direction. And he is calling for backup going the other way. He thinks he is following the suspect. Plus, when I fell in my car, I pushed out all the buttons…I wasn't on any frequency."

Now the officer was feeling angry. "I'm very angry. I got angry in the car. Because this guy had done what he did and I felt like...if he could do this to me, you know...I'm a cop...he's supposed to submit to my authority. He's supposed to let me take him into custody because I'm a police officer. I'm more than your average citizen...and if he does this to me, what's he going to do with the next person? So I got really angry and then even angrier. I punch in my buttons. I see nothing. He's disappeared. Where'd he go? I see him in the middle of a mud field. I put out, 'Here he is.' "

At that point, the officer observed a patrol vehicle from a neighboring city turn the corner. With his spotlight he saw the suspect trying to get out of his car. He started thinking again about what he would do if the suspect came at him again. The officer was in great pain and felt the blood coming down his face. He was confused because he didn't know how it got there. He could only drive with his right hand, his left being completely incapacitated. He saw the other city's officer exiting his car and approaching the suspect vehicle. (It was later discovered that this officer thought that a person had driven too fast for the wet conditions and had spun out into the mud field. He was approaching the suspect with the intention of assisting him.)

The wounded officer called the other officer back. "I've been shot," he told him. "That's the 211 suspect and I'm on my way to the hospital.

"I turn on my siren and I'm out of there. I have everything going through my mind...if I get to the hospital, everything's going to be OK....I'm talking to myself, telling myself to slow down at the intersection, look both ways...I can't afford to get in an accident...I'm OK...."

This officer demonstrated what all who wear the badge strive for during a potentially lethal encounter. The officer never stopped thinking, planning, and adjusting to an amazing series of frustrating circumstances that left him without communications with any other law enforcement resource. He refused to accept defeat. He had practiced often in the past, and in many ways, to prepare himself for these few seconds of his life—in order that his life would continue. He had come up against a very dangerous man and had won.

The suspect bled to death from a chest wound incurred in the officer's first return of fire. In my mind, the officer was truly a hero, not because he took the life of a felon in a violent gun battle, but because he did whatever it took to prepare himself for effective combat. He didn't become lazy or complacent with the mental preparation required for officer survival; his brain never went into withdrawal, which we'll discuss shortly. He never went into shock, because he kept concentrating, thinking, planning, and prioritizing what he had to do. He kept himself moving, acting, and never ceased his efforts against the obstacles to his victory over grave threat. The officer is a working police officer, today a sergeant. Not surprisingly, he doesn't like it when his radio transmissions get covered.

This Wasn't Supposed to Happen: Preventing the Psychology of Defeat in a Tactical Encounter

Not every officer possesses a dominant, competitive, "refuse to lose" personality he or she can call upon to ensure victory during a felonious assault. Indeed, I have witnessed, during "simunitions" training with unanticipated assaults against them, officers falling down and stopping any aggressive action when a paint ball struck them—even when the paint ball had struck them in the arm, shoulder, or leg.

The "fight or fight" response is properly understood to refer to human survival instincts in response to an extreme threat or trauma. There is, however, a third instinct or action often taken by human beings who encounter situations: freezing.

Most human beings (except for those employed in law enforcement or the military) are simply not mentally or physically prepared to engage in combat as their response to an encountered threat. The majority of human responses will likely be either passivity or an attempt to withdraw in order to escape the threat.

Police officers, conversely, are trained and *expected* to overcome normal, instinctive human needs for self-protection—and to advance toward a threat to end it in a decisive manner. When new officers have successfully passed the Academy and field training, they expect to win tactical encounters because, they believe, they have practiced using all the officer safety principles and tactics they were taught.

They have been permitted to keep engaging in the same field problem until they achieve success and victory. It is, therefore, a huge shock when they are in the field and an assailant gets the upper hand and stabs, shoots, or bludgeons them. The thought that comes to the wounded officer at this moment is often: "This wasn't supposed to happen!"

Unfortunately, however, the skills learned in Academy training, the expectations developed by Field Training Officers, and the desire of the individual officer cannot always be expected to overcome the brain's instinctive response to an extreme threat. During circumstances in which an individual is forced into a position of helplessness (or, more accurately, when the individual places him- or herself in a position of disadvantage), he or she may experience feelings of helplessness, isolation, or defeat.

For the officer to survive, he or she must overcome a human survival instinct that has existed as long as there has been predator and prey: the instinct of "conservation withdrawal." Historically, the initial, primitive mechanisms for the survival of organisms under grave threat have involved an instinctive quietude. By becoming and remaining still and quieted, the organism does not attract predators or predatory assaults against itself. Think, for example, of two dogs in combat. One achieves domination and begins to defeat the other to a point where the defeated animal's life is imperiled. The defeated dog will often stop its fighting and lay on its back in a submissive posture. The submissive, passive posture serves to communicate to the aggressor the end of aggression because a threat is no longer posed.

When Your Bubble of Immortality Is Burst
He was the type of officer who is referred to as a "statistics whore." He had a competition with his Academy mate to see who would get the Automobile Club's award pin at the department's awards banquet each year for the most grand theft auto (GTA) arrests. He had about four years "on the job" and was an aggressive go-getter who was consistently the most active on his watch.

His sergeant had counseled him about his performance. "Hey, I'm pleased with your activity levels, of course," the sergeant had said. "But wait just a minute. You got dragged down the street for a block and a half last week with your head and shoulders in a suspect's vehicle while fighting the driver for the ignition keys. What's up with that? I'm pleased that you're motivated to get the most GTA arrests, but I don't want you hurt getting them, do you understand?"

"Don't worry, Sarge," the officer had countered. "I made the arrest when that guy was dragging me down the street with the stolen vehicle, didn't I?"

Up to that point in his police career, he hadn't known defeat. Indeed, he introduced himself to me as a "street fighter...able to take care of whatever business comes down." He looked down on those officers who were less active, and who did not work like hunters. He called them "slugs" or "lames." He thought they were afraid. He never could see himself doing police work like they did.

It was an early morning or "graveyard" shift. The officer was heading southbound on the main thoroughfare in his town when he saw a vehicle pass him going northbound. He locked eyes with the driver and immediately "smelled" auto thief. He quickly performed a U-turn and began to follow the suspect vehicle. When his position dictated he could do so, the officer "lit up" the suspect's vehicle with his forward-facing red lights to order the vehicle to halt. Instead of pulling over, however, the suspect attempted to evade, and pressed his accelerator to the floor in an attempt to distance himself from the officer. The officer engaged in pursuit.

The vehicle pursuit became a foot pursuit when the suspect had a traffic collision. The suspect attempted to "get lost" in an uninhabited area containing no lighting, steep embankments, deep gullies, and scrub terrain. The suspect fled down the side of a steep embankment into the darkness. The officer was now faced with an unanticipated change in the tactical situation. In this situation, an experienced and wise officer might have called for backup assistance. He would have called for canine resources and helicopters. In short, he would have called for all the resources available to assist him in pursuing a dangerous suspect.

For the young, aggressive officer, however, such actions would have delayed his pursuit of the suspect, and allowed the latter to evade apprehension. That option was not acceptable to this officer. He lived by the simple rules of those in police work whose "bubble of invincibility" has not yet been burst by cold reality: "When you run from me, I apprehend you. I take you down. My task is to get as close to you as I can in order to prevent you from succeeding in your attempt at flight. I will catch you and I will take you to jail."

Without any hesitation, the young, brave, and aggressive officer charged down the steep embankment into the darkness. But the officer had now placed himself in a position of disadvantage. He was unable to see the terrain he was maneuvering in and there was insufficient light from his flashlight (even if he had taken the time to take it from his radio unit) to enable him to see what was in his path. He tripped upon some unseen obstacle and fell.

The way in which the officer fell caused his arms to be trapped on each side by the sides of a small crevasse he had fallen into. The suspect leaped upon the officer and began pummeling his face and head with fist blows in order to move the officer's hands away from protecting his service weapon in its holster.

The officer was now no longer the officer-as-hunter. He now needed to defend himself.

The officer instinctively fought to control the grip area of his service weapon to prevent its removal from the holster while he was on the ground. The officer was conscious and aware of his circumstances. He knew that he could handle the assault against him. He thought to himself: "I can handle this. I'm a tough guy. I have taken stronger punches in the face than this guy is throwing, and kicked butt. I can handle this."

Then he took a horrific blow to his face, much harder than he had taken earlier, and more fierce than he could feel confident in withstanding. He forced his eyes open (through the blood already caking his face) and saw that the suspect was raising a large rock with which he had struck the officer in the face to strike him again. Now the officer's conscious awareness of the threat he was confronted with contained a very different tenor. He now felt that the scene was "too much for me." He felt a sapping and loss of his strength.

These feelings were new to the officer. When he saw the suspect raise the rock to strike him, he felt defeated and helpless. These feelings frightened him and he said something he would never have imagined himself saying to a resisting suspect: "OK, you can go. My job was to catch you; your job was to get away. OK, you win...you can go...." But the suspect didn't go. He told the young, now frightened and injured officer: "No, cop...I'm going to stay here and I'm going to kill you." He then brought the rock down on the officer's face and head again and again. (The officer sustained five cranial fractures during this incident.)

At this point, however, the "cavalry" arrived. While the officer had not responded to radio calls, he had radioed in that he was in pursuit as soon as the pursuit was initiated. The officer's patrol vehicle had been spotted with its driver's sidedoor open and lights on. The sergeant who had attempted to counsel his young stallion now called out to him to answer, in a voice filled with alarm and urgency, asking him for his location.

To prevent the officer from calling out to his comrades, the suspect covered the officer's nostrils and mouth with his hands. When the suspect's hands cut off his airways and ability to breathe, the officer felt terrified. His panic at being unable to breathe restarted his fight for his life, and he survived.

The officer has returned to work a wiser man. He may or may not get the Automobile Club award pin. But, what is certain, he will be more likely in the future to be a safe officer who picks his battles on his terms and for his advantage.

Prior to this incident, the officer had never felt the need to train or condition himself specifically for the purpose of maintaining the will to fight and survive. Because he had never lost, a pattern had been developed in which he perceived himself as an aggressive, courageous, victorious, and successful police officer. He expected to win every encounter he faced. Therefore, when the unthinkable occurred and he was rendered helpless by the circumstances he had "dived" into, he was without any familiar, automatic reflex response.

While police training does, of course, refer often to "the winning attitude" and "the will to survive," it doesn't yet address how an officer keeps a winning attitude when the officer is isolated and feels defeated and/or helpless. There are a great many law enforcement officers working today who have never taken a punch to the face prior to their employment with a police agency. What experience base would they have had "to fall back on" when they are unexpectedly made a victim of a felon's vicious attack?

The answers to this critically important question are reasonably straightforward. First of all, human beings are creatures of habit. Habituated patterns of behavior become automatic responses. As previously stated, _the brain will do as it has practiced. It will not do what the officer hopes will happen, it will do as it has been conditioned to do._ Repeated practice with service weapons permits officers to respond without delay or hesitation—analyzing the situation and planning what to do to save themselves or another. The use of their service weapon has now become a conditioned response and is performed automatically. Their response to threats against their safety is a sequence of actions practiced over and over again.

For this training and practice to succeed, however, it must be applied immediately—and forcefully—in the face of a threat. If police officers are fearful, hesitant, and/or passive in the use of the tools of force they have been trained in and practiced with, the tools will not work. Threatened officers are then faced with a fight for their life without effective resources with which to protect themselves. If officers also experience a psychology of defeat, the result may be fatal.

It obviously does not make sense for an officer confronted with a lethal threat to take the time to stop and engage in conscious analysis ("Now let me see…they're drawing a gun, they're pointing it at me…I see a muzzle, I am in grave danger, am I justified to use lethal force because of fear for my life?"). Such mental activity will obviously result in a hesitation that places the officer in grave danger.

Many police officers today are just not psychologically prepared, predisposed, or comfortable in putting a resistant or threatening suspect down immediately. Too many police officers permit their perception of themselves as providers of community service—or because of a fear of punishment—to limit their use of aggression when responding to a threatening suspect or subject. The tendency for officers to delay and/or avoid aggressive action in order to prevent consequences they may face has appeared, for example, in law enforcement in the aftermath of the infamous incident involving Rodney King in Los Angeles. Since then, many officers have expressed the feeling that it is necessary for them to use hesitation and/or "let things happen" in order to avoid being the defendant in a lawsuit.

The expectation of punishment or consequences if the officer uses force and/or aggressive action creates a conditioned response in the officer's mind. The officer develops an association between the immediate and decisive application of an aggressive response and concerns or fear that negative consequences could befall him or her for doing the job. How many times does a person burn his or her hand by putting it on a hot stove before becoming nervous about approaching a stove?

Officers I have interviewed who successfully defended themselves against lethal assaults have reported that they were competitive individuals and did not accept losing at anything. They were mentally and physically ready when the threat was encountered. The others are dead.

Being Prepared

She was in civilian clothes and was driving home from her assignment as an Academy tactical instructor in her personal vehicle. Two male and two female gang members in a car had been following her for thirty miles. One of them had a .357 Magnum pistol he had stolen from his mother. It is likely that the gang members who were stalking a lone female guessed they had a relatively easy victim to take. When the off-duty officer entered the driveway to her home, the car filled with the gang members followed. A male and a female got out of their car and approached the off-duty officer.

As the officer was stepping out of her vehicle, she noticed that the male suspect had a gun in his hand and was pointing it at her. She always kept her own gun handy (think of that when you lock your gun away in a glove compartment or attaché case off duty!). As soon as she saw the suspect, she identified herself as a police officer. And as soon as she identified herself as a police officer she was shot in the chest by one .357 Magnum bullet from the suspect's weapon. She returned fire at exactly the same instant she became aware she was being shot. When the first four bullets from the officer struck the suspect, he retreated to the rear of her vehicle. He attempted to continue shooting at her but was stopped by her vigorous counterattack. She discharged a number of shots into him and ended the threat.

When the officer saw that the suspect was down and had stopped attacking her, she turned and headed for the entrance to her home. She now realized she was bleeding profusely from a chest wound and knew she needed to get help right now. The amount of blood loss was severe, however, and she collapsed on the driveway. As she recalled, "Everything faded to black."

Her roommate was in the house and had heard what sounded like firecrackers outside. She saw the officer down, and immediately called "911"—notifying dispatch that she had an off-duty police officer down, shot and bleeding on the driveway. Her next call was to their neighbor, another police officer in the same department as the downed officer.

The neighbor responded immediately and observed first the officer lying on the ground, bleeding, and then a dead juvenile behind the second car. Remembering an in-service training class he had attended on first aid for gunshot wounds, the officer placed compresses on the wound on her chest to stanch the flow of blood. She was dying. When they arrived, paramedics put a compression suit on her. They lost her pulse and got it back twice.

The suspect's bullet had nicked the officer's diaphragm, taken pieces of her duodenum and colon, pierced her kidney and spleen, and put a hole in her heart. She was given emergency surgery at the hospital and placed on life support. However, she was losing too much blood, so the medical staff realized that she was still bleeding somewhere inside.

The surgeon approached her and, by hand squeezes, the wounded officer acknowledged that she understood the medical team was going to have to perform another surgery immediately. However, because it was only an hour since the first emergency surgery, the team could not put her under general anesthesia again. During the second surgery her heart went into full arrest.

The doctors now put their hands inside her and massaged her heart. They discovered another nick in an artery that was the cause of the continued bleeding and repaired it. Fading, the officer was placed on full life support. Her family was brought to her and stayed with her. They kept talking to her. "You've never been a quitter," they said. "You've never quit. Don't quit now. Don't give up." Officers and staff who worked with her, or who know her in her work with other officers as a tactics instructor and instructor in the will to survive, later learned what her family already was banking on: This woman never, ever quit. Miraculously, she survived, spending one week in an intensive care unit.

The officer was transferred to a monitored ward for seven to eight days more. Fifteen days after this most serious injury involving two major surgeries and being technically "dead" a number of times, she walked out of the hospital with no medical restrictions. She spent eight months doing her own rehabilitation, because, as the officer explained to me, the medical team "didn't know how much I could do." Eight months after being shot in the chest, this brave woman was back at work on full and regular duty.

The officer participates in a class called, "I've Been Shot: Maintaining the Will to Survive" sponsored by the California Narcotics Officers Association. She was asked during one of the sessions if she remembered what she felt at that moment when she realized she was being shot: "Very angry," she replied. "Because I had 'I.D.'d' myself as a police officer and he still shot me. How dare he not respect what is right? How dare he not respect law enforcement?"

A number of officers who survived gunshot wounds they suffered during assaults have described their belief about what it takes to maintain the will to survive. They unanimously describe the importance of the continuous mental preparation they underwent prior to the encounter. They say they had conditioned themselves for what might happen to them and what they would do if struck. They determined they would "deal with the pain later....Now's the time to survive," they said. Furthermore, they expected to win. They did not permit personal difficulties, relationship problems, fears of departmental or media scrutiny upon their work product, or fear of punishment for using lethal force to limit or govern their aggressive response to a threat.

Officers need to realize that pain is no barometer of how badly you are hurt. If an officer is unprepared mentally and physically for a life-or-death struggle, then the pain and shock of being struck by a bullet could well result in conservation withdrawal. It is these officers who are likely to die.

The officers who say to themselves, "I'm too tired for my workout tonight...it'll feel much better to get a couple of beers and sit down in front of the TV," and who, therefore, submit to the feeling of fatigue or discomfort, are in reality training or *conditioning themselves to be defeated*. Fatigue or complacency have been more powerful an influence upon the officer than the commitment to program, train, and *condition him- or herself to overcome all odds*. A pattern begins to develop in the brain that will submit to fatigue, pain, or discomfort, resulting in some degree of surrender. When, therefore, such an officer is shot, stabbed, or bludgeoned, the entrenched habit patterns will not be those that achieve victory.

Sources of Compromise to the Will to Survive

I have observed three primary influences upon the loss of positive mental attitude in police officers over the course of twenty years of service to law enforcement. The first is police depression and anhedonic behavior; the second is conservation withdrawal; and the third is an expectation of negative consequences or punishment—i.e., feelings of defeat for using force against threatening suspects.

1. Police Depression and Anhedonic Behavior

Police depression is completely different from depression experienced by civilians. Civilians get depressed because of neurotic (maladaptive) responses that are inside themselves and their relationships with others.

Police depression, however, is anger officers experience and direct against themselves subsequent to their experience of helplessness. Helplessness refers to the inability of the officer to impact and control a contact the way he or she felt the need to. Things that *happen* to the officer are what cause police depression. It is not a result of some flaw or weakness in the officer's mental and emotional makeup.

Police depression shows itself as self-defeating or self-destructive behaviors: "Aah, I'm too tired....I don't feel up to exercise and exertion....I won't do my workout tonight. I don't care. It'll feel much better to have a couple of beers, watch TV, and relax." The first thing to go when an officer is depressed is his or her vital energy, physical training, and mental and emotional conditioning.

Many police officers, if they were honest with themselves, would acknowledge that they've stopped doing things they used to do that strengthened them. They would acknowledge that they don't pursue their hobbies or favorite activities as they used to. They don't feel that vital energy they began their career with. They feel tired even after rest. They stop wanting to go out of the house after work. They fail to react positively to their children's or spouse's entreaty for attention.

Anhedonic behavior is the opposite of pleasure seeking or hedonism, and refers to a withdrawal from an individual's activities that normally provide strengthening, pleasure, and feelings of normal well-being. When police officers allow themselves to be controlled by their fatigue and/or lack of desire or energy to work out, physically train, and maintain top condition, they are conditioning themselves for surrender. Sometimes the time to work out the most is when you feel like doing it the least. You cannot be stopped. No amount of pain or fatigue or loss of energy can overcome your will. Officers who perform in this manner will conquer all obstacles. They cannot be defeated—they just will not permit it.

The pressure on police officers to be in control at all times and never fail in their duty is enormous. The burdens of failure can lead to anhedonic depression, which in turn impacts the will of the officer to survive.

Police officers will very often judge themselves a failure when they have, actually, arrived too late to have prevented the harm they've encountered. Many officers find themselves feeling a loss of energy and drive in the aftermath of incidents in which they felt a great need to impact some circumstance but were unable to do so. They may blame themselves for something they were helpless to impact and then begin to engage in self-defeating activities. The officer is, therefore, confronted with a choice. Either she or he does whatever is necessary to continue the process of developing strength and mastery, even in the face of temporary defeats, or she or he allows fatigue, reactions of distress, and negative emotion to defeat her or his strength and will. It is, quite simply, a matter of life and death.

2. Conservation Withdrawal

As noted earlier, the term "conservation withdrawal" refers to a quieting or ceasing of aggressive action because of a primitive survival instinct that arises within the psychology of defeat. Conservation withdrawal is the term that refers to an individual or organism shutting down aggressive action, becoming passive or "quieting" in response to a threat that is perceived as overwhelming or defeating. As noted earlier, if the officer perceives a threat as overwhelming, the officer's brain may cause the body to shut down in an attempt to conserve itself. If the individual has the perception of mastery, purpose, and potency in the encounter, and is properly conditioned for the threat, the shock reaction will not occur. If the individual perceives mastery, purpose, and potency in the encounter, he or she will not go into conservation withdrawal. Rather, the officer will be aroused to the degree necessary to vanquish the threat that was made against him or her.

3. Expectations of Negative Consequence

In a national study on Police work stress,[2] it was reported that sixty-four percent of all police officers expected to be punished if they did their job. A similar percentage of officers reported their belief that the stresses they encountered in their work would prevent them from completing their career.

Litigious individuals and risk managers' "bean counting" appear to have created a reluctance on the part of administrators of police agencies to perform training and maintain policies that might be considered in a court as predisposing officers to aggressive action. Policies have been written that make officers jump through procedural hoops in order to justify aggressive action in defense of themselves. As it is, suspects have enough advantage over police officers. The officers' own neglect of efforts to pre-program themselves to survive and be victorious ought not to be another advantage police give up in order to avoid punishment.

Violence isn't pretty. It is extremely shocking and unnerving to the naive citizen. It's an uncomfortable truth, but the best way to trigger a life-or-death combat intensity in an individual is not terror alone but hatred and rage. It may look nicer to see officers as "Officer Friendly," to be sure. But, and this is a *big* but: If the police force creates an impression in officers that avoidance of vicarious liability is more important than the officers' lives, then law and order is surrendering to criminals and abandoning the innocent people who depend upon the police officer to save them from the danger that, unfortunately, continues to exist.

The prevailing social attitudes and climate in which today's police officers are scrutinized and judged have had the effect of creating a hesitation or passivity in police officers to signals of threat that might have been quickly extinguished prior to the incident involving Rodney King. And we continue to lose police officers.

I do not accept that there is an acceptable casualty rate for police officers. We must swing the pendulum back a little, away from the excessive reluctance on the part of police commanders and politicians to have law enforcement personnel be viewed as anything other than the happiest, nicest kind of people we can know.

Officers, I believe, must continually and consistently, as the adage goes, "act the best, hope for the best, and prepare for the worst" in developing their attitudes and demeanor when confronting subjects or suspects. Those things that are most important to the officer are the things that make him or her strong and unwilling to surrender: loved ones, unmet goals, unfinished living. All these are examples of what it is that officers fight for and want to return home to day after day.

Officers must pre-program themselves, therefore, to act decisively and aggressively to avoid becoming victim to a felon's bullet, knife, or bludgeon. If their department does not provide such training, conditioning, and development of appropriate, pure, and righteous aggression against the criminal, then police officers must do this work themselves. There is no other option.

An investigator assigned to the Texas Narcotics Control Program approached me during a speaking engagement on surviving undercover stress. He expressed concern for California-area police officers, and told me to tell them that, in his opinion, "It's better to be judged by twelve than carried by six."

How true those words ring.

---

1. See, for example, California Law Enforcement Officers Killed and Assaulted in the Line of Duty, 1990–1994 Report, pp. 1–47.
2. Blum, 1998.

4: Living with Guilt:
Cops who Survive Other Cops Who Were Killed

There is a promise to be kept in police work that goes as follows: "If you need me I will be there. I will risk my own well-being, even sacrifice my life to get to you. I will forsake the comfort of my home and family—for we are partners." Such is the bond that exists in the police family. Inability to keep that promise causes officers great suffering.

Lives Lost...Lives Changed

Two officers had been dispatched to a call about a male transient seen loitering in the driveway of a residence in town, and information and a description were broadcast about the man. One of the officers (whom we'll call Officer M) had just recently returned to patrol duties from a three-year special assignment in narcotics. An officer who was not on-scene but had heard the radio transmission (whom we'll call Officer G) knew the subject being described by dispatch from previous contacts. The subject was, Officer G knew, a homeless person who often created a public nuisance. Officer G decided to respond to the call to assist the two officers assigned to the call; he believed his knowledge of the subject might be of help. There was also nothing else happening that night.

After getting the subject to move on, the officers stood and chatted for a moment. Officer M then stated that he was going to go and check a vehicle he had observed prior to getting the call. Nothing was unusual about Officer M making such a comment. For a moment longer, Officer G and the officer who was the cover officer for Officer M remained at the scene where they had asked the transient to move on. There then came a "shots fired" call from dispatch, with Officer G as the handling officer and Officer M as backup. Officer G responded to the dispatch transmission and Officer M did not. Officer G did not think the lack of response by Officer M was that big a deal.

Dispatch then put out that a citizen had called in about a police unit with its lights on in the middle of the street. A roll call was performed and Officer M did not respond. Now nervous, Officer G went to the street where the police unit was observed, and saw a police vehicle with its lights on. Officer M was down on the ground in front of his car with a crowd gathered around him. Officer M was conscious.

Officer G could see that Officer M was bleeding. He asked his fallen comrade: "Do you know who I am?" Officer M responded that he did and gave him a brief description of the perpetrator. Officer G was now in a quandary. As he told me later: "I wanted to help him. I wanted to do something...I didn't know how. There was too much blood....I wasn't qualified....This wasn't normal. This was personal...."

As he recounted this horrific experience many years later, Officer G's breathing became rapid and shallow and all color drained from his normally ruddy complexion. He was reliving the pain of helplessness he had experienced when he stood over his fallen comrade and couldn't do a thing to help him.

After an eternity of waiting, medics came and Officer G accompanied Officer M in the ambulance to the hospital. While in the ambulance, Officer M kept trying to push the oxygen mask off.

When they arrived at the hospital, Officer G had to change out of his uniform and put on scrubs to go into the operating room. Investigators came. Officer G stepped outside the operating room as the doctors operated on his friend. He told the investigators everything he remembered seeing, hearing, and doing.

"I got the impression that it was bad," Officer G told me. "But I thought he was going to be OK. He was talking when I first got there and he knew me. I got the feeling he was going to be OK."

Officer G went to the recovery room after a while and asked for Officer M. A nurse turned to him and told him in a matter-of-fact tone that Officer M had died. Officer G spent some minutes at Officer M's bedside. He broke the cardinal rule demanded of police officers. He showed emotion. He broke down in tears. Officer G was driven back to the department in the scrubs he had put on in hospital. He understood the good intentions of the other officers who took him back to the department right away. He wanted to get back into his uniform. He walked into the department in hospital scrubs and felt out of place. Although he didn't know it yet, his experience had now set him apart from the other officers.

"I felt like some strange bug...the way I felt and the way they all looked at me...like, 'What are you doing here?' When I talked to the shrink I told him I was *okfine*. I just think I didn't know how I was. I just gave the standard answer." (Note: The term "*okfine*" can be translated as follows: "My guts are burning. I can't focus. I feel like a truck just hit me. I think I'm going to throw up. I'm not telling you a thing, Doc. If you want to know what I feel, read my mind. I'm *okfine*.")

The day after Officer M was murdered, another officer approached Officer G and informed him that a fire captain had reported that the medics believed Officer G was dazed and confused, as if he didn't do all he should have done. The officer told Officer G that all "the guys" believed he had done all he could have for their fallen buddy.

Officer G then began the process that has especially injured countless police officers who have lost a partner—he started second-guessing himself. Had he performed properly? he wondered. He felt stymied about what he could have done at the scene to help when he first saw Officer M bleeding. The comment made by the fire captain had opened up a dreadful door to questions about whether he had performed as a cop is supposed to: "That comment has damaged me to this day. It served no good purpose," he told me.

After he finished writing the supplemental reports he was responsible for, Officer G and his buddies went out drinking. They told stories (read: "lies") to each other as a way to sort out what had just happened to their buddy that changed them, their department, their world, and their lives. He went back to work the next night.

"I had a great deal of anger," Officer G told me. "Piddling calls. [I felt:] 'I just had my partner die and you want me to care about your silly problem?' I was basically all right until a 'shots fired' call was broadcast. I pulled over to the side of the road because I couldn't stop shaking. I told the sergeant and took a couple of days off." Everything started to feel odd, unreal, and not the way it should be. Nothing felt normal anymore to Officer G.

One night, a couple of weeks later, after driving around aimlessly in his patrol unit, he saw another unit go by. He could have sworn he had just seen Officer M. Later, he walked into the briefing room and saw Officer M there. Driving past the geographic location of Officer M's murder, he looked up the street and saw a radio unit parked with the lights on. He turned and went up the street to take a look. There was no unit there.

He couldn't go to management for help: "They'll think you're losing it," he said to me. "They'll say, 'Give me your badge and gun.'" He spoke to a buddy of his, a guy he could trust, but he still kept a lot of what he was going through hidden from anyone else. The other officer didn't know what to do with what Officer G was telling him.

Officer G then came up with the idea that he was no longer in love with his wife, and moved out. It was at that point that Officer G realized he needed help. "I had completely changed how I worked. I no longer looked for things. I'd just stop and have coffee. I started drinking a lot. I changed friends and started going out with the drinkers because I didn't feel out of place with them."

Officer G was not yet grieving for himself, for what he had witnessed and lost. He worried and obsessed about his performance. Was the fire captain right?

"Something's wrong," he said to me. "I'm not the person I used to be. I loved this woman, now I don't. I don't work the same, I'm a different person. It had to be M's death.... Doc, it was very disconcerting to realize I had lost who I was."

He has often dreamed of the scene in the years since M's death. "I still see the same image...the unit sitting there with the lights on...M down....Freeze frame....Over time it's been less painful to remember."

He is confused about how the incident could affect his feelings for his wife. She is a gracious, loyal, and good woman who has now borne them a child. He couldn't see how the two things could be related. However, the connections made sense when he learned about survivor's guilt in the work he did in therapy. He had been protecting himself from feeling any feeling on the one hand, and on the other hand he was punishing himself for the fact that he'd been helpless. (As the officer and I were going through this interview, tears were running down our faces. Both of us had learned from the consequences we had lived through; both of us had learned because we'd withdrawn from loved ones; both of us had rejected life's gift—to protect ourselves from feeling the pain and to punish ourselves for our helplessness.)

"My wife and I were separated," Officer G said to me. "You were telling me things, but I didn't accept them. I was convinced I wasn't in love with her—that it was over." They went to separate marriage counselors. Officer G took the time and effort needed to sit and think about his life for real.

"I'm miserable without her," he told me. "I was happy with her. With treatment, it dawned on me that it wasn't just at work that M's death had affected me."

He started dating his wife again. It took time for them to get comfortable with each other, because he had left. He finally made the decision: "I'm unhappy where I am, I was happy with her. I asked her, 'Let's go back.' We did a western wedding in Vegas…got remarried.

"There was elation with us falling in love again. We got off on our own again. Work is no longer the breath of life. To this day, I say 'If they didn't pay me, would I be here?' No. I'd be home with my wife, where I belong. I still try to do my best (while on patrol) but it's not what I'm on this earth for."

In the Aftermath of a Murdered Police Officer

In few other occupations does the violent death of a co-worker generate such severe and generalized injury than police work. Other surviving workers don't even have to have known the deceased officer to go through substantial grief, trauma, and shock in their thoughts, moods, emotions, and interactions with others.

Police agencies describe themselves as a "family," and how true this is is clearly seen in the aftermath of officer deaths. Some families grow closer in grief. They support and help each other through the processes that are consistently experienced along with the death of a loved one. The members of these families often come out of their loss in a healthy manner. They create positive personal goals and a good outlook for their future by their realization that, as they may say, "Life is too short. I'm going to live a more quality life for whatever time I've got."

In other families, the grief a family feels can be infected by unresolved family issues that had nothing to do with the death of a family member—but which get "dumped" into how the family copes with their loss. The anger some family members had for each other prior to the death are often inserted into their reactions to the death and create what is called a *pathological grief reaction*. Finger-pointing, attempts to place blame for things they feel helpless about, and flare-ups of conflict over necessary tasks are some examples of dysfunctional means of dealing with grief. Family members may do this because they are not used to feeling so out-of-control. They may feel that by pointing the finger at someone's actions or lack of action, they'll be able to make some sense out of what has just happened to their world. They may, of course, have no reason at all.

"Should It Have Been Me that Died?"
A violent gang member, armed with a machine gun, had murdered an officer. When officers in a two-officer unit—part of a street robbery suppression team—had confronted the gang member, a serious and fatal gun battle had occurred. The murdered officer was well-liked and capable. His surviving partner was female. She worked as a decoy. She would dress as a poor woman and sit on a bus bench and wait for a crook to attempt to take her off. Then the police force would move in. Physically short of stature, she was young and filled with the vigor of life.

The officers worked in a busy area; there were gangs and narcotics and street crimes to deal with. The officers in this station were "tight": to be respected and accepted as a good cop, an officer had to prove him- or herself. The male officer had done just that and was popular and well liked. His partner, however, had not passed the "test" yet, although she certainly worked very hard as a police officer. It was she who had been driving their police vehicle. She had never dreamed she would experience anything like this. She felt it was unreal. She and her partner had been jogging together; they spoke to each other about all the things partners talk to each other about. She had been horrified by how immense her feeling of helplessness had been when her partner was hit and she had seen how badly he was hurt. She could not shake off the scene: the sight of her partner lying dead in her arms, the smell of gun battles and death, the sounds of the sirens and radio as other officers raced to the scene, and the feelings. This image was locked into her brain.

In the aftermath of the shooting, word got back to her that some of her "family" of fellow officers were blaming her for her partner's death and had made the following devastating comment about the incident: "____ died because she was his partner...it should've been the bitch that died."

It's difficult to find forgiveness for the officers who made such statements in the aftermath of the murder of their friend and brother officer. I'm going to believe they didn't know what they were saying because of their grief and rage at their friend being so violently murdered. The dead officer's partner had no way to make any sense of this comment other than to fill herself with feelings of guilt and inadequacy. For many months after the murder, and every time she thought of her murdered partner and friend, the comment came back to her: "____ died because she was his partner...it should've been the bitch that died."

"Were they right?" she asked herself. "Did I cause that to happen? Did I not do something I could have or should have done? Should it have been me that died? Should I die? Is that how the scale gets balanced?"

In the aftermath of the Vietnam War, survivor's guilt was talked about quite a bit. Survivor's guilt comes about through the pain an individual feels at the helplessness they felt in failing to prevent the loss of persons close to them. Survivor's guilt can be seen also in civilian life. A child, for instance, may have had an argument with his or her parent shortly before the parent's death. Soon after the shock and disbelief of the death is experienced, the son or daughter may begin to feel—instead of helplessness and loss—anger directed against him- or herself for somehow having been responsible for the parent's death. The child will not be able to give a valid or logical reason why he or she is responsible for that death. He or she will simply feel that way.

The murdered partner's best friend comforted the female surviving officer. He understood there was nothing she could have done to prevent the loss of his best friend. He consulted with the investigating homicide detectives to find out what the facts were about this incident. He wanted people's reactions to be fueled by the evidence rather than the infection their anger and prejudice created.

Homicide detectives told the friend there was nothing the surviving partner could have done to save the murdered officer. She had, they said, in fact done a good job given the circumstances she and her partner had confronted. The friend told the officer repeatedly what he had found out, and that it wasn't her fault. While she greatly appreciated his care and the support these comments gave her, the feeling did not go away. Every time she thought about the incident, that comment kept burning inside her. It is now eleven years since the death of her partner, and she has never fully shaken off her sadness. Nevertheless, she has two beautiful children born to her and her husband. God gave her back life for the one he took from her.

When a Cop Dies: Stages in the Grief Response

Most people think of grief as a relatively short-lived feeling. We expect to feel grief after the death of someone dear to us, because it is logical to grieve for a short period of time. The expectation is that once some time has passed, one continues on. There are formal rituals in every culture to facilitate this process of grieving.

What many people do not realize about the grief reaction is that it has no schedule by which it works to leave the person in peace to move on with his or her life. Some of the stages in the grief response may not even begin until several months have passed since the death has occurred.

A number of studies have been conducted about death and dying in an attempt to understand how people react to this inevitable passage. The studies have found that there are some fairly predictable stages of grieving that people are likely to go through, and that there are some predictable problems that people may experience in these stages of grief.

Stages of Grief

If an individual experiences a death that was unexpected, the individual's experience of grief will be more severe than another individual who was close to a dying person. The murder of a police officer is always unexpected. The individual has no way to prepare for the loss in the way a family can by talking with a sick loved one and "finishing" emotional business. It is highly likely that the grief process law enforcement goes through when one of its own is murdered is more severe and more prolonged in duration.

The experience of shock, the feeling of disbelief, and that sense of a loss of reality are likely reactions for members of a police agency, for the first few days up until the funeral. Some people stare off into space, then laugh, thinking about a funny experience they had with the deceased officer. Then they will cry for a while.

Officers go off to the local bar and drink beers and talk about experiences they shared with the fallen officer. Telling stories and sharing experiences with other officers is of great benefit. Repeating the experiences they had with their deceased partner helps surviving officers to begin to absorb what has happened. At that moment, the death hasn't sunk in yet. The first few days in the immediate aftermath of the murder of an officer can feel a lot like a rollercoaster ride.

I usually tell officers, dispatchers, record clerks, cadets, jailers, sergeants, lieutenants, captains, and chiefs to think of the shock and disbelief many of them feel in the first few days as a gift their brains give to them. The long-term reality they will live with hasn't hit them yet. The world they have lived and worked in has, all of a sudden, stopped. They may be numb and feel they are only "going through the motions," but what is happening is that the brain is softening the blow of what has happened to their partner.

Officers may find themselves wandering aimlessly around the department or their house. They may forget and not finish things they had started to do. They understand the reality of death, but not yet the finality of it. Like Officer G, many surviving partners have reported they are shocked to find they expect to see their partner walk into a briefing like he or she did before being killed.

Another demonstration of police grief I have observed far too often is the acute feeling of sadness and loss at the funeral. This is the one time and place that officers are not chastised for showing tears. Indeed, crying is a logical and very healthy adjustment a person makes to the intense shock he or she has been dealt. Men and women in law enforcement who tend to have difficulty recovering from the murder of a fellow officer (i.e., those who develop long-term emotional or mental distress and/or are observed to be engaging in self-defeating or self-destructive behaviors) are those who cannot or will not allow their body the *normal human adaptation response* of tearfulness.

These are sometimes the officers who are excessive in their efforts to help the widow, widower, parent, children, or fiancé(e) of the murdered police officer deal with all the responsibilities and business of carrying on without their loved one. It should be understood that, while self-control is a good thing, if officers control themselves to the point they become rigid or inflexible about how they feel, their healing may be arrested.

When the reality that his or her partner is not coming back hits the surviving partner after the funeral, a heavy, depressed feeling may descend upon the survivor. Appetite is often lost; sleep can be disturbed. What may be influencing this weighed-down feeling is that the immediate support and attention paid to officers and their feelings by so many sources of support has ebbed or ended.

Many officers who do not directly express their feelings of grief express them as anger. They may become irritated with their loved ones. One such officer related: "They're going on about their lives as if nothing has happened to stop them. I can't do that because the world I knew doesn't exist anymore. It pisses me off when I see them go on and then expect me to be the same. I can't do it." Such an officer often complains to me that he or she feels abandoned by loved ones, who are not being thoughtful and considerate of how the officer feels. The feelings these officers are describing are actually their experience of loss displaced or transferred onto something that may be more familiar to them or something that is easier for their coping mechanisms to deal with.

When people are feeling either physically or emotionally distressed or when their feeling of distress disrupts their activities (in the aftermath of death), they may be unaware that it is the death that is causing them to be uncomfortable. (In psychological jargon this is called *denial*.) What usually happens is that the officer will experience the internal distress, focus his or her attention upon some currently occurring external irritant, and judge that the source of the discomfort is a reaction to whatever it is that's irritating them. This is why many grieving police officers "snap" at their children, spouses, life partners, etc. Others begin to speak bluntly or insensitively about colleagues or their department. It's not just an issue of the officer being in a "grumpy" or "pissed" mood. The officer's irritable and angry reactions are justified in his or her own mind because, as he or she might say, "People are pissing me off. If they wouldn't piss me off, I wouldn't get angry."

When police officers' reactions begin to change from shock, disbelief, or rollercoaster emotions into anger, they are actually experiencing post-traumatic shock. What this means is that the incident has temporarily overwhelmed their normal coping mechanisms. This type of shock is a logical and probably necessary part of the grief response in police officers. An officer has, however, to be alert to the real reasons he or she is no longer reacting in the accustomed way. Many surviving partners have told me: "I changed. I wasn't that same person I used to be anymore." Of course, these officers *are* still the same person they've always been. But their point of view has clearly been altered by the trauma of their experience.

In addition, officers may start to feel that the things they used to find so important to them have lost their meaning. They may experience bitterness, especially toward those who don't show an appreciation for the loss they are going through. Indeed, I warn police officers that they may experience flare-ups of temper or irritability when citizens speak to them in an irritating manner at a traffic stop or when they respond to a call for service. I tell the officers that those who offend them are not worth worrying about. I tell them not to give these people the power to cause them to lose their cool.

It is astounding how many surviving partners leave their marriages that never had problems before the murder (as was the case with Officer G). Others end intimate relationships they were happy with, while others go to another police department. The way I have been able to understand the phenomenon of officers wanting to leave previously fine relationships is, again, as follows: Officers have to protect themselves from feeling any feeling on the one hand, and on the other hand punish themselves for the fact they felt helpless. I believe that if the relationship you're in is the right one, you do everything necessary to fix the problem. My late father, no believer in psychology, used to say that the definition of mental health was easy: "It's when you get pissed off at someone but you can forgive them."

Almost all the officers I've worked with in the aftermath of the murder of a partner have had, to some extent, a feeling of pain at what they are going to miss in the future because of that loss. It's as if the officers now view their future life only negatively. While this is a logical reaction for them to have, they must be aware of the real source of that feeling.

It should be noted that the pain is not merely emotional. Many people who grieve over the loss of loved ones—especially those who have a tendency to bury their emotions—develop real physical pain and distress that is actually "converted" grief. Chest pains, the feeling of one's heart pounding out of one's chest, headaches—all are examples of physical distress reported by surviving partners.

Many officers experience premonitions of what the future is going to offer them. But it is conceivable that what they are actually experiencing is a memory. They are feeling the effects of the loss while looking to the future with their thoughts. They feel the pain of loss, look into the future, and see only loss ahead of them—loss that is in fact a memory, something that's already happened.

Too many police officers have "carried baggage" from traumatic events into the rest of their lives because they viewed the world from the perspective they had at the moment the traumatic incident impacted them. Indeed, this is the way in which officers are likely to experience a post-traumatic stress disorder. If you drop a rock into water the only portion of the water traumatized is equal to the size of the rock. With the passing of time, however, the ripples from the trauma affect an ever-widening area. Too many officers have brought themselves many more losses than the loss of their partner by believing their memory was a premonition. The following officer's experience may help serve as an example.

When You Can't Do the Job Anymore
He is now living a good life. His family is very happy because they no longer worry about him every day. But the officer has told me: "Nothing is the same as police work. Nothing even comes close."

The officer is aware that he began to change, to become somebody he'd never been before, some months after the murder of his partner. An armed robber had barricaded himself in a location and officers were in varying positions of cover, scene control, and perimeter containment. The armed robber would not allow himself to be arrested. He had made the decision that he wasn't going to go back to prison. He opened fire and this officer's friend and former trainee partner was shot in the head. There was nothing that this officer could do. He was helpless to have prevented this tragedy.

"I was irritable and short-tempered with everything and everyone around me," the officer told me. "My sleep was disturbed all the time, and I ingested mass quantities of alcohol." He said that he developed a "complete distrust of the public" and the people he worked with. He knew he was feeling quite lonely wherever he went, and felt that a "despair was creeping in there."

He began to have chest pains. The doctor said there was nothing wrong with his heart. "The night they told me to go home, I was getting dressed in the locker room. When I put on the body armor I couldn't breathe. I guess it was a panic attack. That was really scary."

The officer couldn't fathom what the real source of the changes in his life was: "At the time I had no idea. The reason I thought these things were happening was that people in the department were out to get me. I felt let down. I felt no support. I kind of felt that the department wasn't doing what they should have after my buddy got killed."

This officer was highly respected in his department for his skills, character, and bearing. He was not a malcontent or "slug" that expected people to pressure him. "I just liked being a cop. I didn't want to be a supervisor. I just wanted to do my job and go home. Others wanted me to be promoted, and were pushing. Also there were assholes who were supervisors. The younger guys would look up to me and not them. There were always obstacles to me just doing my job and going home."

The officer began to feel that everything he did was now difficult and filled with pressure. Nothing felt right. He had been a Field Training Officer and had felt this a very important part of his work. But that had changed when his friend was murdered. "I didn't want to train anymore," he told me. "I blamed myself. I was one of his training officers. I thought there must have been something I didn't show him—some type of training—so he would have lived. I saw him just the day before. We were talking. I just felt that there was something I didn't say—didn't teach him. I felt kind of responsible. I wish something would have struck me in the head when we were talking the day before, something I might have said that would save him.

"He was working downtown. I was off that day. I worked the same area. I sometimes wish it'd been me. One thing positive: I was on the entry team. At least I got to make entry and make sure the guy was dead. You know, do something." The suspect inside the building had shot himself in the head shortly after he shot the police officer and saw the officer go down. "When ＿＿ died they brought in a psych who explained what feelings we should have. That it was OK to be sad. She told us if we wanted or needed more help we should contact our supervisor. Right. Nobody would. That incident has messed up a lot of people in the department. In the sheriff's academy they told you to suck it up, don't show your emotions, keep them in. They didn't tell us, though, how to release them.

"I called the lieutenant in personnel the next day after they sent me home. I told him the sergeant said I needed to talk to somebody. I asked them for help. He asked me what I needed help for. I had to tell them: 'Because I think I'm going to kill somebody.' I even named a couple of names. That got action. It's just that you have to go over the edge before you get any kind of help.

"I remember going home and talking to my wife. I had a couple of stiff drinks of alcohol. She asked me what I was doing home. It was a week after the heart thing. We knew something was wrong, we just didn't know what it was.

"It was a relief when I came to you," he said to me. "I remember though, I went to your office and told myself: 'I'm not going to tell him anything. He doesn't know a thing about anything.' Of course, five minutes into our talking and everything came out."

There had been a number of incidents that this officer had gone through which had given him some wounds with, and some without, entry marks. There had been an officer-involved shooting when he had first got on the job. His partner was wounded and he got shrapnel. "No one knew anything about debriefing in those days," he told me. "We were back to work the next day."

Talking with me, the officer remembered people he had been unable to help. He remembered how badly those incidents had affected him: "I was supposed to....I'm the police. The scary part was I didn't know what I would do if I wasn't a cop. Like all the guys, I just wanted to go off in the mountains and be a hermit."

The relationships he had with his family were not infected by his anger. That feeling was primarily directed toward people at his work and the public. He was embarrassed in front of his family. He didn't want to lose face with them. "I had more of a negative impact with them than they had with me. They were very supportive."

The work this officer had to do to heal exemplifies the work many police officers may wish to consider if they experience a similar loss. There was a thread running through all the things that bothered this officer. In these incidents, he found himself helpless to impact the situation. Something terrible was happening or had already happened and there was nothing he could do about it: "I felt I had no control and I needed to be in control. That was my job. All the things happening to my body...my mind...I couldn't do anything about it."

In his first few sessions he would find sweat pouring out of him, although he had never really perspired heavily in his life before this event. He needed a safe place to "open his baggage" and begin to deal with the experiences that were tied to that ugly thread he began to realize was his "Achilles' heel."

Peer pressure stops police officers from talking in front of others about things that are distressing them. This officer, now retired from police work and helping other officers with tactical equipment and protection gear, expressed a fear to me for today's police officers: "I worry about the new guys. They're unprepared for what they're going to face. They don't believe they're not always going to win. They're surprised. They don't prepare for what they need to do if they have an officer down."

Reconstructing the surviving partner's life should be a primary goal for police agency personnel and support resources. If grief reactions are not dealt with directly—i.e., that officers work toward accepting their loss without feeling some kind of survivor's guilt—officers are likely to convert their grief into things such as anger at work or toward the unappreciative public. The alterations in surviving partners' attitudes to their work, their possible change in how they relate to their loved ones, and their physical condition may well be grief reactions that are "cloaked" within whatever they are thinking or feeling or doing.

I have survived all the group of kids I ran with in the Bronx back in the 1950s. I have lost a brother, a mother-in-law I loved dearly, and both my parents. I have stood over the graves of police officers. I hate the pain I feel at the loss of them and the emptiness in my life they used to fill. So, as I said before, I embrace the pain. I do not want it tricking me into feeling worse than need be. I have worked hard at this and have come to accept the fact that these people knew how much they meant to me. Yes, of course I wish I could have had that "just one more" experience with them. But I had what I had. In my mind, it is blasphemous to waste the gift that God gave me in having been with them by believing that I am somehow betraying or abandoning their memory by making my life a blessing and a victory. Enough said.

Injury to the Police Family
One of the major sources of difficulty for the police agency in its response to an officer's murder is the likelihood that it has not prepared for this event. The agency may not have made plans for how to manage the media that pressure people for statements. It may not have developed or allocated resources necessary for an immediate procedural response directed at assisting the organization in coping with this tragedy. In addition, the smaller the agency, the more widely the wounds will likely be felt.

What is needed is an initial response by trauma support resources for all witness officers and surviving partners. Dispatchers will also be in need of trauma response, although they are normally the least likely to ask for help. There are many never-before-performed tasks to be done. The funeral arrangements will need to be made. Larger police agencies or other agencies that have lost their own and gone through the experience can be of great assistance during the first two or three days after the officer's death. The agency's leadership will be held accountable for assistance resources that officers may not even want to use. What is important is simply to bring the resources and let them help the officers who are willing to accept them.

Surviving police officers' families will, of course, also be greatly traumatized by the death of one of their own. Whether officers are aware of it or not, the family of a police officer lives in fear every day the cop goes to work that there will be two people from the department knocking at their door. The children of surviving police officers may demonstrate immature or irritating behavior, or go back to behaviors they had already passed through in their development. This is because they are acting out their fear. Negative attention feels bad, of course, but it's still attention. They may well beg Mommy or Daddy not to go to work anymore.

Open and honest family discussion and the airing of family members' fears and feelings and needs will go a long way toward eventual healing. What police officers and administrators need to keep in mind is that the expression of fear and upset is a logical reaction. (I always refuse to say that what officers feel is normal, because there is nothing "normal" about the murder of a police officer.) It is all right to feel pain when something hurts you. It does not mean you have been defeated. When something terrible happens, the right feelings to have will feel terrible too.

Just because you feel some bad feeling doesn't mean you are doing something bad.

In the same manner that individual surviving partners are likely to be injured by the murder of a police officer, there is likely to be injury to the entire police organization. And all levels and parts of the organization should be urged to take the necessary steps to bring the agency to the goal of reconstruction as well.

5: Use of Lethal Force: Consequences for Police Officers

No civilian—and, indeed, no officers who have not themselves been involved in an officer-involved shooting—can truly understand the unique experience of the split-second decision the officer must make. For an officer, the rest of his or her life is impacted by the decision with *no time* to make it. If you don't shoot, you may never see your loved ones again. If you're passive or hesitate, and the suspect shoots you, stabs you, bludgeons you, takes away your service weapon, or runs you over with his car, the consequences are likely to be dire.

If you act quickly and use lethal force, you will become the subject (or suspect) in a post-shooting investigation and will face possible lawsuits. The media may descend and create a *cause célèbre* from the act you did to save your or someone else's life. If you use lethal force and all you had wanted was for the suspect to comply with your responsible commands but he or she assaulted you, your conscience may do a tap-dance on your soul: "If only I had....Should I have done something different that would have brought a different outcome? Could I have stopped it? Was it my fault? Did I do right? What will my department think about my actions? What about other cops? What about my family?"

"We Killed One of Our Own"

Christmas is a time of year that is supposed to be for family and festivity. December 23, in 1983, however, will be indelibly etched in the minds of several police officers in a busy Los Angeles County police agency. It was on that night that the son of a sheriff's deputy took his father's service weapon and went out after police officers.

The report came out that a youthful suspect had fired several shots at police officers in the open until they returned fire, and then had run. On two occasions, officers in pursuit had been "jumped," or ambushed, and had faced the muzzle of the suspect's weapon. However, the suspect had not fired at these moments, but had run away again.

Both times, each of the pursuing officers had thought they were about to die, and were confused at what the suspect was doing. A foot pursuit ensued, which included patrol personnel and the canine unit. On several occasions, always in the open, the suspect would fire in the direction of the officers. After a number of hours in a tense and unusual pursuit, officers believed they had the suspect cornered in the one-car garage of a residence in the hills above their city. Seven officers and a canine formed an entry team and entered the one-car garage.

The canine went into the alert response at a storage cabinet. The canine handler pulled open the door to the cabinet. (The handler was as concerned as much for the dog's safety as his own.) The handler was confronted by the barrel of the gun held by the teenager.

Thinking that he was about to be shot, the handler dropped to the floor. He may actually have momentarily lost consciousness.

When the six other officers saw their partner and friend fall, they thought he was being shot. The dog was howling. The officers were armed with shotguns and .45 semi-automatic pistols. They were all in a one-car garage. They opened fire at the suspect and continued firing—one of the officers screaming at the top of his lungs as he fired.

The entry-team leader rushed to the side of the fallen officer. The dog attacked him, snarling and biting. The firing stopped. Someone observed physical movement in the suspect and called out, "He's moving!" Another officer rushed to the teenager and fired an additional shot into the top of his head.

This suspect had fired upon officers on a number of occasions. He had ambushed two officers and had turned away and run. He had pointed his gun in the face of an additional officer at point blank range but had not fired. This was an extremely dangerous situation.

The officers were taken back to the department. The association attorney was called. The captain ordered the officers to give reports of what they did. The association attorney told them not to give any statement. The chief of police and a captain questioned them in a manner they perceived as critical, asking why they had done what they did. The attorney told them not to speak to the department psychologist as he feared the psychologist would serve administrative concerns more than those of the officers.

The canine handler and one of the officers who had been ambushed by the suspect—both of whom thought they'd been going to die that night—decided they needed to talk to a shrink about what happened to them. One by one, in private, these veterans of urban police work began quietly to communicate to me their shock and extreme distress at the fact that the suspect they had taken the life of was a cop's kid. They considered they had taken the life of one of their own. They could not help but wonder repeatedly if there had been anything different they could have done to prevent the outcome.

In addition to this concern, the canine officer continued to experience the shock, fear, sense of great danger, fear of loss of his loved ones, and an imminent belief he was about to die—which he had felt as he opened the door to the storage cabinet. His feelings and perceptions did not go away, even though he had distanced himself in time and space from the incident. His contact with the suspect at the storage cabinet had created a shock reaction that had rigidified—or locked in—all the different physiological emergency reactions, perceptions, thoughts, and feelings that had occurred at that split-second in time and space when he believed he was about to die. They had not gone away, even though the threat had ended.

The entry-team leader had recently suffered the death of his father, with whom he had been very close, and had recently separated from his wife. He had experienced extreme distress when he saw the canine officer go down, as he thought that the canine officer had been shot and that he would lose him as well.

The officer who had been screaming as he continued firing at the suspect had been in an officer-involved shooting three months prior to this incident. In the previous incident, a gang member had been shooting at a rival gang member in a crowd at the county fair. The officer had had to use lethal force to stop the gang member, who was running and shooting. The bullets entered the suspect's back and the gang had sworn revenge upon the officer and his department. That same night, shots had been fired at police officers' homes, and the officer blamed himself for the threat to other officers. In addition, he had developed a severe and ongoing hypersensitivity about possible lethal contact. This had exploded inside him on December 23, 1983.

Each of the officers in that garage had varying degrees of concern about other circumstances external to the threat they encountered that day. These concerns at varying times and to varying degrees had preoccupied them as they became involved with taking the life of a cop's kid.

At some point during the next few weeks, two of these officers developed severe post-incident stress reactions that did not subside. These reactions began to affect them in patrol duties, domestic relationships, and in their own mental, emotional, and physical condition. At other points over the next several months, still other officers who had been in the garage began to experience an extreme level of dysphoric, or distressed, reaction, as well as distortions in their perceptions of circumstances in both their personal and work lives. Four out of the seven officers who entered the garage eventually left their planned careers in police work.

The use of lethal force is the ultimate enactment of authority by a police officer. An incident has to fit within specific policy guidelines promulgated by each police department in order for lethal force to be appropriate, a policy that is scrupulously engineered to meet the specific requirements of the department's jurisdiction. The use of lethal force is automatically investigated by the homicide team of the officer's own agency (if the suspect and/or officer is killed), as well as by a shooting review board and/or the county's prosecuting attorney's or sheriff's investigators.

The use of lethal force must be justified to the officer's supervisors, departmental commanders, the inevitable media attention, community and special-interest groups, and to the officer's peers and him- or herself. While the legal test for justification of lethal force by police officers varies by jurisdiction, the basic elements can be summarized as follows: Legitimate use of lethal force by police officers requires that any reasonable person with the training and experience of the involved officer would have perceived lethal threat in the actions taken by the suspect.

Impact Upon the Officer
None of these jurisdictional or legal tests get to the heart of the crucial decisions and feelings that an officer experiences in a potentially life-threatening situation. Not only must the officer worry about an immediate threat, but there are always questions about the consequences of using lethal force. What will happen to you if you shoot? Will the department support you? Will the jurisdiction you work for simply settle with the suspect's family merely to save on legal fees? Will the department "hang you out to dry" in order to cover itself from negative media and/or community "watchdog" groups? Will the department be sensitive to what you just went through and show you support, or will you be treated like a suspect? Will your spouse or loved one comprehend what you went through and what you need after this incident? If you are killed, will the city

support your spouse? What will be the impact upon your life of being involved in this, the ultimate test of a police officer?

Some shooting incidents can make an officer feel heroic, and these present no negative or harmful after-effects. Indeed, statistics gathered by Psychological Services of the Los Angeles Sheriff's Department[1] suggest that approximately a third of all officers engaged in an officer-involved shooting report no negative reactions following the incident. Another third of responding officers report moderately severe but short-term after-effects (called post-traumatic stress reactions) following their shooting. However, another third have prolonged, severe symptoms that are resistant to extinction.

Indeed, even where an officer does not experience distressing post-trauma reactions during an on-duty incident, he or she may still experience some significant perceptual distortions. These distortions are caused by an abrupt "shift" in the area of the brain where maximal amounts of neurological activity occurs.

Many officers have reported such perceptual reactions as a slowing motion during encounters with a lethal threat. We have already discussed the reasons why the cerebral cortex takes a longer amount of time to register what the eyes are sensing. Suffice to say, the part of the brain that registers what the ears hear loses a great deal of neurological "spark and fuel," so officers' perception of sounds such as gunfire are often reduced to a point of muffled "pops" under emergency conditions. Likewise, such a change also means that the brain finds it has to work harder to consciously recognize or "register" what the senses are observing.

When an officer pre-judges a call because he or she expects one circumstance but finds another, the shock can lock in the feelings of the moment of impact in the officer's memory long after the event has ended. Thereafter, even when the officer is able to distance him- or herself from the incident in time and space, the senses, thoughts, and feelings occurring in the officer at the moment of impact will be maintained in a rigid manner well after the incident has ended.

As we have seen, the officer may relentlessly second-guess his or her reactions. It is logical to expect officers to question the adequacy of their tactical response; indeed, such questioning and debriefing are how improvements in tactics and training are made. However, when an officer experiences perceptual distortions in incidents in which he or she experienced momentary helplessness or loss of control, there is a danger the officer will view these distortions as "evidence" that he or she "screwed up."

The tendency to critical self-judgment is made because police officers are not often trained with knowledge about the perceptual trauma that occurs during encounters with unanticipated or uncontrollable threats to their lives. They believe in the validity of what they see, hear, smell, think, and touch. The problem occurs because often the only thing a cop can trust and believe in are his or her senses. It is perceiving (through the senses) that tells the officer what he or she is encountering and what the officer needs to do to survive and control the situation.

When There's Nothing Else You Can Do

A call was received on the "911" line at a police agency that a male suspect was breaking the windows of a strip-mall shopping center with the butt of a rifle. The officer handling the call had three years' experience as a police officer and maintained a natural command presence. He was a weight-lifter and a competitive and aggressive individual. He was accustomed to taking control of situations with ease. Indeed, he had never responded to circumstances where he could not immediately take charge.

When the officer arrived at the scene, he observed a man seated on the curb and holding a rifle with his hand on the barrel, the barrel facing straight up in the air. The man's head was down and he made no movements of any kind.

The officer had placed his car between himself and the suspect, had his driver's door open for cover, was wearing his body armor—mirrored sunglasses, helmet, shotgun drawn with round chambered—all of which combined to give the officer the feeling that he had effective insulation and distance between himself and the suspect.

The officer told the man to place his weapon slowly on the ground or he, the officer, would be forced to take action.

The suspect's response to the officer's presence and verbal command, however, was *weird*. Never taking his hand off the barrel of the rifle or moving his hand toward the butt or trigger area, the man slowly lifted his head. More slowly still, he began elevating his body until he was standing erect, facing the officer with a "thousand-yard stare" locked onto the policeman.

To his dismay, the officer looked into the suspect's eyes and realized, in his own words, that "the lights were on but no one was home." What, in fact, the officer was seeing was the stare of a man whose girlfriend had earlier left him for another man, and who had resolved to get a police officer to kill him so his girlfriend would pay the price of guilt. He was, at the very least, not going to cooperate.

The officer again tried further verbal commands on the suspect, telling him again and again to drop the weapon and obey his commands. The officer wanted this confrontation to end without violence; he wanted neither himself nor the suspect harmed. The suspect's reactions were, again, *weird*. Never taking his hand off the barrel of the weapon, never changing the direction in which the weapon was pointing, and never removing his rigid, locked stare from the officer's eyes, the suspect slowly began to walk toward the officer.

Now the officer became fearful. He felt a sense of imminent threat, urgency, anger, and an awareness that chilled him. He had lost control over the situation.

A second officer now arrived to back up the first. Because he had not seen the events that had transpired and had no idea what the first officer was experiencing, his perspective was quite different. It ran something as follows: "I see we have a person with mental difficulties. I'll wrestle him down in an assistance-related manner, take the weapon so he doesn't hurt anyone, take him to the County Mental Health Receiving Unit, who will dump him back out onto the street in four hours as no longer a danger to himself or to others, and everything will be *okfine*."

When the suspect observed the approach of the backup officer, he swung the butt of the rifle into his underarm area in a firing position and aimed the barrel at the second, oncoming officer. That is the moment when the first officer let go a shotgun blast in an attempt to save his partner's life. The slug caught the suspect underneath the shoulder and the suspect dropped like the proverbial sack of potatoes. The threat appeared to have ended.

However, when the first officer had observed the suspect turn to threaten his partner, time appeared to slow substantially. The suspect was turning incredibly slowly toward his partner, raising the barrel of the rifle equally slowly as he turned. When the suspect had earlier begun to approach him, the first officer's feeling of being under great threat, his sense of urgency, and his perception that he had no impact upon the suspect's actions had "freeze-framed" in his mind. He had experienced a shock reaction, in which the moment he experienced the feelings of imminent danger, fear, and the inability to impact the danger remained with him even though the objective threat had gone down. Thus, when he shot the suspect, the first officer continued to experience great fear, great and imminent threat, and felt that he had *to make him stop*! These frightening and helpless feelings remained at an intense level even after the suspect was down.

A sergeant had now arrived at the crime scene and observed the first officer's actions. He had no idea what this officer had experienced but now observed the officer moving aggressively toward a body on the ground. When the officer reached the suspect, the sergeant pulled him off the downed suspect and, with a look of disgust, took the officer's shotgun and service weapon from him. The sergeant did not observe (or did not care about) the look of shock upon the young officer's face. He placed the officer in the rear seat of his radio unit (usually reserved for criminal suspects) and silently drove the officer to the police department. The officer was sequestered in a room alone. Other officers were ordered not to have any interaction with the officer until the homicide unit finished its interview.

Crime scene technicians placed plastic bags over the officer's hands for purposes of testing gunshot residue. They did not let the officer wash the blood of the dead man off his hands. (Now, more than seventeen years later, this officer, on reflection, admits that he still feels the blood of this man upon his hands.)

Every twenty to thirty minutes, someone's hand would appear with a cup of coffee and then go back out again so as not to contaminate the investigation. The officer heard someone say in the hallway, "Hey, did you get the suspect's blood?" Then the crime scene technician came into the room and told him they would have to take his blood.

The officer reacted badly. This was how you treated a suspect. He had shot a guy who appeared to have moved so slowly that the officer secretly questioned whether there was anything else he could or should have done. He secretly questioned whether he should have been physically able to do many more things before shooting. What else could he believe? The guy had been moving so slowly and the officer had felt a loss of control. He must have screwed up. The department must have thought he screwed up. Otherwise, he reasoned, the department wouldn't be treating him as if he were a suspect.

He felt even lousier when he was told that the suspect's weapon had not been loaded. He was experiencing secondary traumatization, brought about by the apparently complete absence of concern for him by his own department. He felt horrible—that with one short incident his life had changed completely.

The officer became angry. Why are people messing with me? he thought. When the officer was debriefed by the department psychologist, he was able to describe how angry he was at the way he was treated in the investigation. He was neither able nor willing to acknowledge the fact that, several hours after the incident, he continued to experience the same perceptions, thoughts, and feelings he had felt when the suspect had locked a dead-eyed stare on him, had slowly begun to walk toward him, had raised his rifle into firing position, and aimed it at his partner.

The officer never told others about the fear he began to feel when he went back on patrol duty. He began to experience a specific type of fear of assaults by suspects and subjects, since, he felt, any situation could create the possibility that this nightmare might happen again. When he was forced by circumstance to make traffic stops and the subject began to mouth off to him, the officer put them down. Hard. There and then. Physically. In his mind he had resolved never to give anyone the opportunity to make him feel that helpless again. Whereas the officer was beginning to realize that his feelings of threat and fear were tied to the shooting, there appeared to be nothing he could do about it.

Today, this officer, one of the best at law enforcement, continues to experience the effects of a shooting he was involved in years earlier. In those instances of lethal contact where an officer experiences unanticipated shock, perceptual distortions, or traumatized emotions, the aftermath of the incident may exert a greater and more harmful impact upon the officer than any threat he or she may encounter in the field.

Traumatic and Non-Traumatic Uses of Lethal Force

Three primary elements appear to determine how an officer will respond to lethal threat. First, the characteristics of the incident itself will impact the officer. If the incident, for example, involves an armed robbery, and the suspect is shooting at other officers or innocent citizens, the officer is likely to feel no major negative reaction in his or her use of lethal force. Indeed, he or she may be treated like a hero. In situations like this, the circumstances are clear-cut, understandable, and agreeable to all witnesses to the event, and the officer does not experience feelings of helplessness or loss of control.

In some types of incidents, however, an officer is placed in a totally different set of circumstances. There are examples such as a "suicide by cop," where (somewhat like the individual in the study above) the subject is too cowardly to kill him- or herself and makes the officer do it—something that occurs more than most people realize. As we have seen, the incident may haunt the officer, as he or she has no desire to use lethal force. The officer is forced to shoot by the actions of the suspect.

Countless varieties of situations exist where officers torment themselves with endless self-critical commentary, as their feelings of helplessness transmute into feelings that they have, somehow, indefinably, erred in their tactical response: a gang member attacks an officer with an automatic weapon and turns out to be fifteen years old; an officer goes to a routine domestic disturbance and someone is hiding under the bed and starts shooting at the officer with a shotgun; a fellow officer is shot and killed, and the officer arrives too late to save him or her.

The second primary element of impact upon officers in lethal-force incidents involves the way the officer is treated by the department, his or her loved ones, his or her peers, the media, and the courts. In the study above, I called this "secondary traumatization," and it is difficult to conceive of the amount of damage that has been done to officers by it. The procedures used in post-incident investigations, reactions to officers by their commanders, the manner in which officers' loved ones react, and media sensationalization have all resulted in substantial—and totally preventable—damage to police officers.

Conversely, I have witnessed actions by chiefs of police that have created positive, healthy adaptations in officers, simply by the fact they provided sincere and visible support to those who had just faced death. Several departments have initiated trauma support teams comprised of officers who have themselves been involved in fatal shootings and who provide initial support to involved officers. In these departments, post-incident trauma reactions have been not just lessened, but eliminated. It is tragic to think of how many officers have experienced severe Post-Traumatic Stress Disorder (PTSD) that could have been prevented relatively simply or extinguished by the proper response to the officer.

Following uses of lethal force the officer is immediately responsible for an explanation of his or her actions. If officers are able neither to predict nor understand why the investigative process they encounter is being used, they may well feel that they are being treated as if *they* were the suspect, *they* had done something wrong.

The manner in which a post-incident investigative process is performed can help or hurt an officer, making the recovery from the incident either more simple or more difficult and prolonged. The following may go through the officer's mind: "I cannot recall all the elements of the shooting incident. I experienced an apparent slowing of time and motion when I saw the suspect turn to point the weapon at me. The department has just read me my "Miranda" rights. Do they think I'm dirty? Is their action evidence that they think I'm to blame? If they're treating me like a suspect and I can't quite make conscious sense out of what happened to me, I must have screwed up. Oh shit, now what will happen to me?"

Finally, the officer's pre-event personality characteristics, as well as "excess baggage" the officer may be carrying prior to the incident's impact, have shown substantial influence in the ways in which officers adapt to those incidents in which the use of lethal force was required. Officers who were preoccupied or distracted by frustrations and/or irritations prior to their involvement in the incident appear to have a more difficult time responding adaptively to post-incident encounters than officers who were free of worries, frustrations, and stresses when they experienced the incident.

Officers have often expressed confusion about what reactions they should expect to experience following their use of lethal force. Many have questioned why some instances of lethal force are experienced as extremely traumatic to some officers (such as those incidents resulting in PTSD), while other instances have resulted in no post-incident stress reactions whatsoever.

One of the most telling influences upon whether or not an officer experiences trauma is his or her ability to prepare psychologically for the encounter. The officer who expects to arrive four to five minutes after a suspect has left a bank robbery call (due to the normal delays in transmission from the time of receipt of a call by the dispatch center), and who instead is fired upon at point-blank range by the armed, fleeing suspect, will have a greater likelihood of being traumatized by this incident than backup officers who have been informed that officers are in a firefight and are taking rounds.

This is because the backup officers have been psychologically prepared to be in an encounter involving lethal force. They have a greater likelihood of being able to use a tactical plan and are less likely, therefore, to be placed in a reactive and unplanned or unintended tactical position. This is not to imply that backup officers will not experience distressed emotional reactions to a fellow officer being attacked. Rather, the point being made is that these officers will be less likely to experience a shock reaction to the use of lethal force than will officers who could not psychologically prepare for the use of such force.

In addition to encounters with unanticipated elements, a major causative influence in officers' experience of trauma during lethal-force encounters is the existence of prior instances of (traumatic) lethal force they engaged in.

Each One Is Different

An example of a veteran police sergeant's experience with situations that continually called for lethal force provides a vivid explanation of the effect that *prior* lethal force incidents have upon subsequent officer reactions: "My first shooting was probably every cop's dream," a sergeant told me. "I caught two armed-robbery suspects. One of them shot me in the chest with a Mac 10 submachine gun and my vest stopped the fatal round. I killed that suspect and exchanged rounds with the other one. When it was over I was a hero who had survived. I never realized how stressed and keyed up I was until several hours later. It was then that a veteran cop hugged me and told me that I did a great job out there. I can't describe the relief that came over me to hear those simple words. Why hadn't someone told me this sooner? Would I have continued to stay stressed and keyed up if nobody had told me I had done a good job out there?

"My second shooting was six months later. Two ex-cons were committing a burglary at 3:00 a.m. in an alley. I was alone and the suspects spotted me. One suspect dove for cover while I drew down on the second. I shouted commands and orders over and over, but this guy wasn't listening. He was looking for cover and to see if I had backup. This suspect had three avenues of escape away from me when, suddenly, he made his move. He crouched and began to run for cover—only not away from me. He was running in my direction and at the same time his right hand was going inside his jacket.

"It all happened in a matter of seconds. I continued to yell and scream: 'Stop, freeze, freeze or I'll shoot.' But at the same time he was pulling out a black butt of a gun from his right front pants pocket. I shouted over and over: 'Freeze, freeze, freeze, or I'll shoot.' And suddenly he is within a foot of cover and I fire, wounding him. The gun turned out to be a stolen radio (pocket size). The suspect had been drinking and was no doubt going to get rid of the stolen property. I had shot an unarmed suspect. This was a clean shooting and I had no problems dealing with it until five years later.

"Five years later, I found myself chasing another robbery suspect. I had information that he was armed and that the gun would be in his waistband. As the suspect ran closer to a dark alley that would give him the advantage, he made the move for his waistband and I fired, knocking him to the ground with a wound to his legs. I cuffed him and frantically searched for the gun in his waistband...it wasn't there. 'Oh shit,' I thought, 'I've shot another unarmed suspect magically reaching for his waistband.' I searched more frantically, and found the gun further down his pants. What a relief! But then I found out that this wasn't the suspect I had been staked out for. It turned out that this was another unlucky robbery suspect who had decided to commit a robbery at a market that the cops had already been staked out on.

"All the other cops knew that this was a clean and good shooting, but I found myself being eaten alive with guilt from within. The only thing I could do was continually criticize myself for everything I had done that night. I kept telling everyone, 'I'm *okfine*, I'm *okfine*, I'm fine.' But I was a mess inside. I couldn't sleep...my mistakes wouldn't go away. I continued to criticize myself over and over and over.

"The next day, I couldn't take any more and I called a friend that had been through this before. This friend knew what I would be feeling, and I told him that I was screwed up and needed to talk. I needed help! We met the next morning and I told him exactly (every deal, every detail) what had happened, and how bad I felt.

"My friend told me that it was a great shooting and my decisions and reactions were perfect. I told him not to lie to me. We went over every detail again and again and again, and I began to see [that] what I did wasn't so bad. In fact, the more we went over it, the better I began to feel. The next day I actually began to feel proud. I had made a good observation, my reactions were consistent with the threat, and I had made a good arrest of a really bad guy. My best decision of all was to call that friend the next day."

What this officer didn't realize is that the source of the distress he experienced after the third shooting was not *caused* by the elements that he and his buddy went over in such detail. It was, in fact, a *flashback* of the doubts he had felt about shooting a suspect who was armed with a pocket radio. They were, in fact, a nonvisual memory of the feelings he had experienced when he became the defendant in a wrongful death trial involving this incident. (The jury rightfully believed his sincere belief that his life was in imminent danger.)

However, as I have discussed, since police officers are trained to repress, or "stuff down," conscious awareness of internal self-doubts and/or anxiety, the sergeant experienced these memory traces *as if they were being caused by his third shooting, five years later.* His guilt feelings and self-doubts were projected or transferred to the currently occurring circumstances, as if it were these circumstances in which his bad feeling made him believe he had somehow "screwed up."

As described so eloquently by the above-quoted sergeant, an officer will usually not be cognizant of the fact that he or she is having a type of memory (i.e., flashback). Rather, the officer will likely project the source of his or her reaction into the present time by believing that it was caused by some part of the currently occurring incident. Such flashback phenomena have been responsible for officers sometimes experiencing upset reactions to incidents that might not by themselves have elicited such reactions.

The first days after a traumatic incident can be an emotional and mental rollercoaster. The officer may expect a number of symptoms or reactions to present themselves. Of course, nothing suggests that an officer is going to experience post-trauma stress reactions. However, two thirds of all police officers are likely to experience at least moderate levels of post-incident stress reaction for the first seven to fifteen days following a trauma.

As we have seen, part of the cause for post-incident stress is due to the characteristics of the incident itself; part of the cause will be due to how the officer is treated by the department, co-workers, family members, and the media; and part of the cause will be the officer's pre-incident personality, mood pattern, and family history (children of alcoholic and/or dysfunctional families will have a higher likelihood of post-incident reactions).

Here is a list of reactions that may occur during the first three days following a lethal-force incident:

- ◆ sleep disturbance; troubled, fitful sleep; arm, leg, jerking during sleep flashbacks of the event while awake
- ◆ physical/mental/emotional fatigue, especially twenty-four hours after the incident
- ◆ depressed appetite; nausea; vomiting
- ◆ headaches, muscle aches, cramping in muscles
- ◆ doubt about the adequacy of the officer's tactical response

- feelings of sadness, crying, or tearfulness at seemingly ridiculous moments
- periods of numbness or withdrawn behaviors
- feelings of betrayal by the department
- fear that others see you "losing it"
- irritability with loved ones; short temper
- feelings of unworthiness
- sexual dysfunction
- feelings of deserving to be punished
- aggressive patrol behavior; "hiding" and/or avoidance of contact

Some of the above reactions are due to the secretion of the body's chemicals and hormones that arouse the individual to decisive physical action. The effect of these arousal-creating hormones and chemicals lasts from twenty-four to forty-eight hours and can influence or cause a disruption in normal sleep, an increase or decrease in appetite, startle reactions or impatience when surprised by something, and irritability with loved ones.

Irritable, agitated, hard-to-relax, impatient, or uneasy reactions occur in officers within the first three days after an incident because the officer's responses are being fueled by emergency chemicals that were stimulated during the encounter with a lethal threat. These chemicals are operating now, however, in situations that don't merit an emergency response. Some officers have become very angry at some comment a loved one makes that the officer may resent. The officer may express the aggression or rage that was actually generated by the incident one to two days previously.

Some of the above reactions are signals that some aspect of the incident has created an after-effect in the officer. Some officers spend the first number of days re-experiencing the incident over and over, as if it's happening at that moment. They usually fix upon some aspect of the incident that may have troubled them. Some officers experience a numbness in which they feel apart from things going on around them. The numbing is a signal of post-traumatic stress. Numbness is not the same as the officers' feeling no distress after the incident; numbness is a deadening of response to the world around them and, as we have seen, this can compromise subsequent officer reactions in a variety of areas of his or her life.

Officers who experienced "freeze frame" after-effects have reported that their patrol behavior and activities were altered after the incident. Others have reported an increased feeling of being threatened in a much wider range of subject encounters than they had prior to the incident. The term I use to describe this phenomenon is **threat hypersensitivity**. This term does not refer to an officer's readiness and preparation for decisive response to stress. Threat hypersensitivity involves errors in judgment and episodes of misperception that have resulted in officers' reacting with greater uses of force than were deemed necessary by supervisors.

Some of the reactions officers have in the first three days after an incident involve a rigid re-experiencing of some sight or smell or perception of slow motion that the officer experienced at the moment that most impacted them. These perceptions are usually brought about by some encounter with unanticipated elements in the incident. With some officers, there is a feeling of loss of control of the incident or some feeling of having no impact on the suspect, whatever he or she does. These perceptions occur at finite and specific moments in the incident which the officer actually overcomes or adjusts to. However, the brain has now a "super memory" of this perception and continues it in the officer's mind even after the contact has ended.

Then, whenever some stimulus has any similarity to the incident's elements or whenever the officer is stimulated by any frustration, feeling of threat, or feeling of being defied (e.g., the child doesn't take the garbage out the first time he or she is asked), the officer may re-experience an emergency level of physiological arousal even though there is no actual emergency occurring. Some of these reactions are caused by the secretion of opioid substances that act as

123

physiological "pain killers," which the body releases during an emergency. Officers who experience periods of numbness, sexual dysfunction, or loss of interest in their surroundings may be feeling the effects of sedating chemicals the body felt a need to release to protect itself from the stress it was under.

The officer should be monitoring the frequency, severity, and duration of post-incident reactions for the first three to six weeks with a buddy, co-worker, loved one, or trauma support resource to ensure that the above reaction patterns are being extinguished. Ideally, the officer will return to normal patterns within three days following the incident. When some shock and/or trauma has been experienced and the officer experiences moderately severe after-effects, the above reaction patterns should be extinguished within seven to fifteen days by individual psychological debriefing.

Signals of Incident Impact Upon an Officer
The most easily recognizable signal that a lethal-force incident has impacted an officer is that the officer shows abrupt changes in habits. The officer's behavior on the radio may change from a calm and professional demeanor to an irritable or impatient response to dispatch communications. Abrupt changes in the pattern of officer-initiated activity are also a commonly occurring signal of post-incident after-effect.

Patterns of officer activity and patrol behavior should be stable and consistent in police officers over time. Officers develop a comfort zone in how they patrol, how often they make stops, how they hunt for criminals, or how they seek to assist local citizens with local problems or concerns. In a national study on police stress,[2] a substantial proportion of officers reported that the effect a traumatic incident had upon them was in the form of changes in how they did their work. Some demonstrated increases in officer-initiated activity, while others showed decreases or appearances of "hiding" so they would have less risk of getting involved in anything major. What such an abrupt alteration in officer patrol habits suggests to me is that some single incident has been sufficiently intrusive to overwhelm the officer's normal coping mechanisms and work habits.

That an officer abruptly changes how he or she works following a visibly traumatic incident is serious—it suggests an injury to the officer's sense of him- or herself as a police officer. It suggests that the officer no longer believes in or feels safe with his or her habits and normal ways of coping with subject/suspect encounters.

The injury is demonstrated by how the officer acts, how he or she makes decisions, and how quickly he or she acts to take appropriate control and command of subject/suspect encounters. Supervisors would be well served by ensuring that substantial changes demonstrated by officers—i.e., they work differently than they did prior to the incident—come about through conscious choice and examination rather than by emotional or perceptual trauma. The officer may be experiencing flashback activity that could well compromise his or her safety and will to survive.

Officers in such situations may change from friendly, group-oriented persons to people who withdraw from police gatherings while on or off duty. Relationships with family members or others close to them may also be impacted by an abrupt alteration in the officers' "at home" personality.

Another common signal is when an officer second-guesses his or her tactics in or after the incident. An officer may have previously demonstrated confidence in his or her abilities and methods in the field, but now seems somewhat indecisive, worrying more about things that didn't seem to disturb him or her before. This behavior is a signal that the officer is likely experiencing recurrent, intrusive recollection of some aspect of the incident that had impacted them. The recollection may not occur in the form of a visual memory at all. Rather, many officers' experience of intrusive recollections of events may occur in the form of distressed or worried thoughts, premonitions of "something about to happen," or "antsy" or uneasy demeanor with subjects that other officers do not feel threatened by.

In my clinical experience, the vast majority of incidents that were traumatic to police officers had this impact because the officer experienced some degree of helplessness or feelings of loss of control, and those feelings stayed with them even after the incident was over. We have already seen the kinds of things that such feelings lead to: self-directed criticism, feelings of anger directed at a variety of circumstances, despondency, a withdrawal from normally enjoyed activity, and a generalized loss of feeling of vital energy or motivation or morale.

Where a police officer continues to experience one or more stress reactions seventy-two hours after an incident, it is very likely he or she has experienced some type of shock reaction that has left the officer in a condition of **hyperarousal**. Officers want and expect unpleasant or disruptive reactions to dissipate and disappear within three days. If they continue, they are evidence that officers are experiencing post-traumatic stress because of their or others' use of lethal force. This is so whether or not these reactions were caused by the officers' involvement in the incident itself or by secondary trauma the officer received from how he or she was treated in the aftermath of the incident.

If, as is unfortunately the norm, the officer attempts to cloak or "hide" the fact that he or she is having a tough time after an incident where force has been used and created trauma, the time and effort necessary to return the officer to his or her former state of health will be significantly increased. Trauma reactions don't just "go away" by themselves. They will most often, however, "go away" with a relatively simple technique developed and used with individual officers called psychological debriefing. (I discuss this in Chapter Eight.)

Individual psychological debriefing is not in any way intended as a critical alternative to group-oriented critical incident stress debriefing.[3] Nevertheless, because officers will likely attempt to avoid disclosure of any embarrassing reactions, the removal of post-incident stress symptoms will, in most cases, require individual work with the officer in addition to any group debriefing.

---

1. See Stratton, Parker, & Snibbe, 1984.
2. Blum, 1994, 1998.
3. A model developed by Mitchell, 1984.

6: Why Police Officers Should Become Skilled in Managing Law Enforcement Stress

Police psychologists have a unique experience in their work that those who practice civilian psychology do not. Police psychologists are the only kind of "shrinks" who have to fight their clients to take care of them.

The tried-and-true methods that officers are most often taught from the Academy onward develop habits in them. As we have seen, one of the habits traditionally taught officers is that they should avoid showing that any circumstance they encounter bothers them. "Learn not to feel it" is the general instruction. "Take it....If you feel, you could show emotion. If you show emotion, you're blowing it. If you blow it by not being in control over your brain and feelings, how can you hope to remain in police work?" This is an obviously correct approach necessary to maintain officers' ability to take control over encounters with potentially dangerous suspects.

As we have also seen, however, there is a price that police officers have paid, and will continue to pay, for the benefit of removing from conscious control any thoughts or feelings from distressing or disturbing scenes they encounter in the field. Many of the problems that are known to compromise the safety of officers' decision-making and judgment develop from how officers manage stress in their life and work. As I mentioned earlier, many police officers get sick and die more often and at a younger age than civilians whose lives they protect and save.[1] The statistical life expectancy for adult civilians in the United States is currently approximately seventy-five years.[2] The risk of illness and mortality for police officers is significantly greater than is the risk data for civilian occupational controls.

Several studies in the literature on coronary and cardiovascular disease have demonstrated that engaging in the performance of police work increases the likelihood of sudden-onset coronary death. The death rate in police officers from unpredicted coronary death after nineteen years of service is 300 percent greater than civilian control groups.[3] In general, when the health of police officers has been studied through research and clinical studies, numerous examples show the following: increases in the likelihood of physical diseases caused by or worsened by work stress; increases in the likelihood of taking greater amounts of medicine to control problems with the gastrointestinal system; and increases in the likelihood of self-defeating and self-destructive behaviors that compromise officer wellness and well-being. Remember, compromises to the officer's feelings of wellness and well-being are dangerous and can interfere with the officer's will to survive.

"Stress" is a word that strikes fear into the hearts of risk managers and pension/retirement system decision-makers. The word can inspire feelings of derision or disrespect in police officers who manage their work without having to go see "some shrink." The word "stress" has been used to describe so many consequences of police work that its meaning is often lost upon those who most need to understand and control it—i.e., the working police officers themselves.

The fact that police work stress has killed more officers than any felon's bullets has apparently escaped the attention of most policy-makers in municipal, county, state, and federal jurisdictions. The lethal threat to law enforcement officers from stress at work occurs in two forms. First, there is the previously stated compromise to police officers' health. Second, many of the causal factors found to have compromised officers' safety and survival involve some type of mental activity. Uncontrolled stress reactions in police officers can be expected to compromise the accuracy and timeliness of their mental activity. Uncontrolled behavioral habits that result from how the officer manages the stresses of his or her work and life can be expected to intrude upon tactical planning and the use of tactics.

When an officer maintains personal control over how he or she manages the stresses of life and work, however, the experience of mastery the officer develops has been shown over and over again in research to have a very positive effect upon the officer's health. Research has documented that personal control exerted in one's work and life reduces the likelihood of the very stress problems thought to be endemic to police work.

Problems with stress occur in the absence of *personal control* or when the individual officer permits fatigue, distress, or discomfort to control his or her actions in response to stress or pressures encountered.

The Stress Response in Police Officers
The positive feature of the stress response in police officers can be seen in two primary human survival instincts. Human beings react instinctively to ensure survival, with reactions dating to prehistoric times. When the individual first perceives a threat, an instinctive constellation of neurological, endocrine, musculoskeletal (physical movement), and psychological arousal occurs that prepares the individual for decisive physical action—whether or not actual physical action occurs. The energizing and mobilizing response of the human being to perceived threat can be described as an **alarm response**.

The alarm response can be thought of as the instinctive mobilization of the body to prepare for its response to a perceived threat.[4] The "alarm" tries to keep the body in balance under conditions of threat or pressure. It accomplishes this task by increasing the levels of physical and psychological arousal in the body.

The presence of actual, imminent physical threat is not necessary to cause the body to arouse; indeed, such triggers can include many circumstances in which immediate or imminent physical threat does not exist. An officer's anticipation of moving to arrest someone can easily move that officer into a state of psychological and physiological hyperarousal. Feelings of urgency or pursuing a suspect (because of the threat to innocent citizens) are almost guaranteed to push officers into a condition of alarm and hyperarousal. Similarly, officers may experience heightened nervousness when ordered to respond back to the station and meet with the watch commander ("Oh shit! What am I in trouble for now?").

The alarm or hyperarousal response has served the evolution of the human species by generating an automatic life-saving arousal response. Just 150 years ago, an individual in the West who survived the dangers of animals or predatory humans or who had had enough food to sustain him and and his family would have called the day a success. Today, while dangers besetting police officers are more likely to be complex in nature, we humans have not biologically adapted to enable officers to face dangers encountered over the course of their careers without damage to their brain and body.

The second instinct crucial to the long-term survival of police officers concerns how rapidly they adapt to the circumstances they encounter on a repeated basis. A police officer can become rapidly conditioned to encounters with commonly occurring conditions (such as day-to-day frustrations or contacts with subject or suspect) or by a single, powerful event that impacts them substantially, such as a traumatic incident.

After repeatedly encountering stressful circumstances, the police officer's brain begins rapidly to adapt, and begins to react under emergency conditions even when no actual emergency occurs. Indeed, the stresses experienced by police officers—and their adaptation or habituation to those stresses—literally alter neural pathways in the officers' brains as a conditioned response to repeated encounters with stressful situations.

Police work stress, therefore, alters the genetic "blueprint" that heredity has programmed in police officers. If an officer maintains effective personal control in managing stress, the neural pathways developed in the brain will continue to generate commanding behavioral responses appropriate to the circumstances being encountered. If the officer, however, allows the experience of worry, irritability, fatigue, discomfort, or distress to control how he or she responds to stress, the brain will develop conditioned responses that result in officer surrender or defeat.

Keeping the Wounds Hidden
On October 27, 1997, at 3:00 a.m. as usual, a police officer got up and started to load his equipment into the trunk of his undercover car. He was a member of an elite federal task force in pursuit of violent offenders. His duty was to find and arrest the most violent fugitives. His task force served an average of thirteen to fifteen arrest warrants each day and the officer was recognized as being very reliable—something that meant a great deal to him. "I was proud of my work," he told me. "But it was taking a toll on my life and my health." Prior to the federal violent criminal apprehension task force, he had worked undercover in a vice squad for five years and then for three years on a street-level fugitive apprehension team.

The officer had been keeping secret the fact that he experienced severe anxiety and panic attacks as he drove home after he left work. The officer felt in control and "normal" when deadly force was an option, but, he said: "I felt out of control when large crowds would gather while we were making entries and effecting arrests. I had a fear of dying and worried about what was going to happen as we searched room by room for suspects."

The lieutenant who accompanied the officer to my office when he finally broke down described him as "my most dependable agent." The officer had consistently demonstrated excellence, professionalism, and integrity in a diverse career. He had worked on a team that was extremely competitive and where there was zero tolerance for any inefficiency or deficit. The officer related: "I could not believe I could feel like I did and hide it so well that no one recognized how sick I had become."

The officer told me that his feelings of anxiety and uneasiness began to escalate more severely during situations that were not controllable. "The symptoms were racing heart, feeling weak, [and] feeling light-headed and nervous, as if I had too much coffee. These feelings carried over into my home life. Once home, I had difficulty calming down. I felt totally out of control and didn't want my wife to leave the house."

The officer's HMO had treated him for asthma, although he had never tested positive for any physical or medical cause for a breathing disorder. The officer, however, continued to have breathing problems, symptoms that he had had since at least 1994.

The officer received a departmental commendation for quality service that was presented at the Chief of Detectives executive meeting. The officer was so anxious he thought he was going to have a heart attack. His heart was racing. He just wanted to run out of there and keep going.

On October 27, 1997, he was loading his equipment into the trunk of his undercover car when, standing at the rear of the car, he just stopped. "I walked back inside my house and told my wife I could no longer go on like this," he told me. "If I had to live like this I didn't want to live any longer."

He was brought to my office, looking like a corpse. The officer could well have become a corpse if he had not lowered the extremely high levels of physical and psychological alarm he'd been living with for several years. His recovery took a long time: "It was extremely difficult for me. At first I was afraid to go anywhere alone or be left alone. I didn't have the panic attacks [he was removed from duty the same day in 1997] but I still had anxiety problems that were getting better. I still feared dying. Any contact with work, however, would put me back five steps. I did not want to have anything to do with my job in fear of returning to the unlivable way I had been. It made me feel like it was going to start all over again. It was during this time I began to realize the price I had paid with my health to be the lieutenant's most dependable detective; the price I was paying to not let the department and my team down; and the price I was paying to be the best I could be."

Fifteen months later, the officer was really enjoying life. "I really love my job," he said, "but I now know I cannot go back into that environment. I gave twenty-seven years of my life to the department, taking pride in everything I did. It has taken its toll on my health; it has taken its toll on my family. Prior to the above, I had never experienced these problems. I had never had panic attacks, never had anxiety problems, and never felt out of control. Now, however, I want to be around to enjoy life as best I can."

The above officer's experience is a good example of why police officers should become skilled in managing law enforcement stress. The officer's symptoms were primarily a result of a conditioned response that had developed in his brain, in direct response to his work activity. Over time, he had lost the capacity to calm himself following the entry, serving of the warrant, or end of his duty watch.

One of the major fuels for increasing psycho-physiological arousal in police officers is epinephrine (or adrenaline). Epinephrine acts by stimulating the central nervous system in the brain. It increases respiration, circulation, and heart rate. If an officer becomes habituated to repeated encounters with stressful circumstances, the officer's body will likely release adrenaline into the bloodstream and brain even when no emergency is actually occurring. When that occurs, blood sugar levels increase, blood pressure goes up, the gastrointestinal system shuts down, and the direction of major blood flow and neurological energy are altered in the officer.

Among the effects observed in the body's preparatory activation are the following:

- increased arterial blood pressure; blood supply to brain; heart rate; and cardiac output
- increased stimulation of skeletal muscles
- increased plasma; free fatty acids; triglycerides; cholesterol
- decreased blood flow to kidneys; decreased blood flow to gastrointestinal system; decreased blood flow to skin
- increased risk of hypertension; thrombosis formation; angina pectoris attacks in vulnerable persons; arrhythmias of the heart; sudden death from lethal arrhythmia; myocardial ischemia (mechanical heart problems); myocardial fibrillation; and myocardial infarction (death of heart tissue)[5]

Two major components of stress are important for the long-term health of police officers: effort and distress. Effort involves elements of interest, engagement, and determination. It means an active attempt to cope, and gain and maintain control over a situation.

Distress involves elements of dissatisfaction, uncertainty, anxiety, and/or boredom. It is associated with a passive (or fatalistic) attitude that comes with feelings of helplessness.

Researchers have found that effort with distress conditions is accompanied by an increase of the release of hormones that both arouse the body and attempt to shut down the body's activity simultaneously (epinephrine and norepinephrine for arousal, cortisol for shutdown of effort).[6]

In studies, effort without distress was demonstrated as a euphoric state, characterized by active and effective coping, high job involvement, and a high degree of personal control over environmental pressures. Not only did this state show increased energy levels, but there was a suppression of the hormones that shut down body arousal.

Conversely, conditions in which there was distress without effort were characterized by feelings of helplessness, loss of control, and giving up. They were generally accompanied by decreases in body arousal and were usually found in depressed patients and occupational workers experiencing "burnout." The fatigue, irritability, agitation, and generalized unhappiness experienced in "burnout" are primarily fueled by increases in cortisol which, as we saw in Chapter Two, serves the body—in part—by fatiguing organs and tissues in order to prevent excessive exertion. Seligman has characterized this condition as **learned helplessness**.[7] A variety of experiments have documented the very important influence of personal control in the human stress response. A lack of personal control was almost invariably accompanied by feelings of distress as well as elevations in the hormones that placed the body in a "fight or flight" emergency condition irrespective of the actual levels of stress present.[8]

Personal control, conversely, has been shown to stimulate effort and reduce negative emotions, resulting in a non-distressed, restorative physiological condition.[9]

Personal control has been defined as possessing the following characteristics:

- ◆ demonstrated ability to change or manipulate an environmental interaction;
- ◆ perceiving one's ability to change or manipulate an environmental interaction;
- ◆ ability to predict an environmental interaction;
- ◆ ability to understand what is occurring within an environmental interaction; and
- ◆ ability to accept the environmental transaction within some meaningful cognitive framework or belief system.[10]

Of critical importance in the relationship between personal control, helplessness, and illness is the requirement that an individual perceive or possess the expectation of control in order to maintain a commanding and healthy physiological and psychological condition. This perception of control is vital in the development of human behavior, and the struggle to attain control is initiated during the earliest years of life. Parents of two-year-old children will find familiar the attempts of a child at mastery over the environment.

In examining the relationship of personal control to health, Frankenhaeuser[11] has established the concept of "unwinding" after stressful encounters. Her results have shown that being able to exercise control in an environmental transaction facilitates the process of unwinding, thereby reducing the toxic after-effects of short-term stress. She has noted that the speed at which a person unwinds after, for example, a day at work, influences the total physiological "load" on that individual. A rapid return to neuroendocrine and physiological baselines (as they were before the encounter with stressors) suggests that physiological resources are "demobilized" as soon as they are no longer needed.

Uncontrollable work conditions, repeated encounters with stressors regardless of attempts to cope with the press of those stressors, and/or traumatic events will require the elevation or "mobilization" of neuroendocrine and physiological resources for longer periods of time. This in turn creates a greater duration of the stress response, with resultant fatigue, dysfunction, illness, and breakdown.

Intense job demands will not, in and of themselves, result in adverse health consequences. It is only when these demands are combined with a person's inability to make important decisions or control the realities of the job that adverse neuroendocrine-influenced health problems are observed.[12]

Elevation in blood pressure prior to and during an emergency event is a necessary and adaptive human survival instinct. Increases in cardiovascular activity assist the individual in effective preparation to meet a physical threat. Indeed, if one were to view the types of pressures and threats humans were exposed to as recently as only about 150 years ago, the blood system's arousal was a very necessary aid to human survival.

While the types of pressures encountered by police officers today—i.e., psychosocial stressors encountered in contemporary society—do not often require decisive and immediate physical action, the human species has not evolved a different response pattern to stress. We continue to become "jacked up" as a response to pressures and stresses even when such arousal becomes destructive to our health and long-term well-being. Being "jacked up" can feel terrific if we are excited at a sporting event, have a loving encounter with friends or partners, or are awaiting some anticipated event. Yet, as we have seen, an extended state of arousal in police officers can be experienced in the form of "antsy" feelings, difficulty relaxing, easy irritation at a variety of circumstances, or feeling physical distress.

Research data[13] have documented that a strikingly high proportion of police officers frequently and on a continuing basis take some form of antacid medication. The range of gastrointestinal symptoms experienced by police officers—such as burning or sour feelings in the stomach, watery, runny bowel movements, spastic bowel, acid reflux—are results of the body's slowing or suppression of the digestive process.

Large numbers of police officers have also acknowledged the continuing experience of musculoskeletal pain, stiffness, or discomfort in the absence of physical injury or trauma. One of the effects of adrenaline upon the body is to increase skeletal muscle tension—a critical necessity for combat readiness or preparation for flight. The increased muscular activity observed in officers' anticipation or readiness for threat results in a buildup of lactic acid and ammonia (the wastes of muscular activity) which further increases the experience of soreness and physical fatigue reported with substantial or prolonged stress.

Still other police officers have reported repeated colds, influenza, and a lowering of previous levels of resistance to illness. This isn't surprising considering that epinephrine or adrenaline suppresses the immune system during periods of heightened arousal. Violanti *et al.*'s data[14] have shown substantially increased death rates in police officers from cancer after nineteen years of service in comparison with civilian controls.

I have suggested that repeated episodes of stress disrupt the neurological and endocrine regulatory systems. Referenced research has documented the immunosuppressive effects of stress—i.e., a lowered immunity to viruses and cancer-causing substances. Findings suggest that abnormal amounts of adrenaline might actually reduce the immune capability of the body.[15]

Police officers are screened for risk of heart disease prior to being hired; indeed, they are selected, in part, based upon their healthy condition. Therefore, the increase in risk for heart disease for police officers as their length of service increases must be considered at least in part an indication that long-term police duties may be harmful to officers' chances for health and survival without a consistently applied technique that can defuse and de-condition the hyperarousal response in police officers.

Increasing job demands are harmful to individuals and lead to fatigue and depression when environmental constraints prevent those individuals from coping optimally with the demands. Stress can be defined as a perceived imbalance between demands and the perceived capability of responding to those demands. Job tasks with high demand and small possibility of control have been associated with elevated myocardial risk. A lack of intellectual discretion at work, particularly if combined with excessive demands, may increase the risk of cardiovascular illness.

While police work does permit degrees of discretion in how officers do their job, there are episodic, repeated, and continuing incidents over which the officer has no opportunity to use discretion and in which he or she has no control. Increased work activity and a lack of control in how the officer is constrained or permitted to do police work may well disrupt his or her ability to use adaptive, intrinsic coping mechanisms and make necessary adjustments to stresses encountered. An individual's inability to adjust adaptively to stress has been shown to increase the risks of psychosomatic illness and increased mortality, an association that increases in severity the longer an officer is employed.

Let there be no misunderstanding or doubt. Police officers experience psychophysiological hyperarousal ("fueled" by the actions of epinephrine or adrenaline and norepinephrine or noradrenaline) on a daily basis.

The signals that an officer can use to identify that she or he is becoming habituated at too high a level of arousal are as follows:

- multiple awakenings from sleep (either with a need to urinate, or with thoughts of work or home during the time when we should be at rest!)
- irritability or impatience without real provocation, especially with loved ones
- inability to remove thoughts and feelings for the victim from the mind, even though the case has closed
- gastrointestinal distress
- despondent, irritable, uncomfortable moods in circumstances that previously did not elicit such reactions
- headache pain; tightness, stiffness or pain in musculature
- inability to relax even in the absence of direct encounter with psychosocial stressors and/or fatigue even after rest
- lapses in concentration and memory.

Officers who condition and program themselves and their activities for health can simply and effectively control stress reactions caused by excessive arousal reactions. Conditioning for health in police officers involves the use of stress management techniques described in Chapter Seven and Eight.

The Stress Response to Single Events in Police Officers
As noted above, the body's survival instincts prepare the individual for decisive physical action. To increase the individual's chances for

survival to an imminent threat, the body instinctively releases additional hormones (most notably norepinephrine or noradrenaline and cortisol), which fuel the individual's emergency response.

A police officer may experience significant stress from a single event when the following three elements occur:

1. The event is sufficiently stressful that the officer's normal psychological defense mechanisms are overwhelmed. In other words, the event "pierces the calluses" that officers develop to distance themselves psychologically from distressing emotions.

2. The event contains unanticipated or uncontrollable elements, resulting in elevations in norepinephrine discharge and activation of the sympathetic nervous system. The individual here cannot use prior tactical planning or intent to manage this incident and is not psychologically prepared for the incident.

3. The impact of the incident remains with the individual in a rigidly maintained manner, beyond the immediate impact of the stressful event.[15]

The term *trauma*, as defined in popular dictionaries, refers to a "startling experience that has a lasting effect on mental life," and, secondarily, to "a body injury produced by sudden force." The term *startle* refers to the act of "frightening or disturbing suddenly, especially to cause to start involuntarily." The verb *to start* refers to the giving of a "sudden jerk or jump, as from surprise."[16]

The Diagnostic and Statistical Manual-III-Revised[17] has defined post-traumatic stress as consisting of a triad of symptoms: **intrusion**, **avoidance**, and **arousal**.

A stressful event can be said to be intrusive when there are recurrent recollections and recurrent distressing dreams of the event. Likewise, the victim can suddenly feel or act as if the traumatic event were recurring, including reliving the experience. In addition, intrusive qualities of stress refer to an individual experiencing visible psychological distress at exposure to events that symbolize or resemble an aspect of the traumatic event, even including anniversaries of the trauma.[18]

Avoidance in single-episode stress refers to a persistent avoidance of stimuli associated with the trauma, or a numbing of general responsiveness (not present before the trauma). Avoidance can be seen when someone tries to avoid thoughts or feelings associated with the trauma, avoids activities or situations that arouse recollections of the trauma, or is unable to recall an important aspect of the trauma (psychogenic amnesia). There can also be markedly diminished interest in significant activities; feelings of detachment or estrangement from others; restricted ranges of internal emotional activity, and/or a sense of a foreshortened future.[19]

Arousal can be shown in persistent symptoms of increased physiological and neurological activity levels (not present before the trauma)—illustrated by difficulty falling or staying asleep, irritability or outbursts of anger, difficulty concentrating, hyper-vigilance, exaggeratedly startled responses, and/or a physiological reaction to events that symbolize or resemble an aspect of the traumatic event.[20]

One of the criteria required for a diagnosis of Post-Traumatic Stress Disorder (PTSD) is that these symptoms last for at least one month. The character of the experience required for a diagnosis of PTSD is identified as follows: The person has experienced an event outside the range of usual human experience that would be markedly distressing to almost anyone. These include: a serious threat to one's life or physical integrity; serious threat or harm to one's children, spouse, or other close relatives and friends; sudden destruction of one's home or community; or the sight of another person who has recently been, or is being, seriously injured or killed because of an accident or physical violence.

Pitman[21] describes the following steps in the pathogenesis of PTSD:

1.) An extremely stressful traumatic event over-stimulates endogenous stress-responsive hormones and neuro modulators; 2.) these substances mediate an over-consolidation of the memory trace of the event, a process we have previously termed "super conditioning" (Pitman, 1988); 3.) leading to the formation of a deeply engraved traumatic memory that 4.) subsequently manifests itself in the intrusive recollections and conditioned emotional response of PTSD.

The operational definition of trauma, therefore, can be described as a rigidification, or "locking in," of whatever physiological, emotional, sensory, or cognitive activity is in an individual at the split second in time and space where the impact of the incident occurs. As we have discussed, the impact of this event is maintained in the mind, emotions, and physical reactions of the victim of trauma, even though the officer distances him- or herself in time and space from the incident. Thereafter, any subsequent elements that "remind" the victim officer of the traumatic incident trigger the re-experiencing of, for instance, a sense of threat or urgency, a feeling of helplessness, a smell, a sight, a look on a victim's face, etc.

While epinephrine or adrenaline serves as a general central nervous system stimulant; noradrenaline is secreted in the face of an extreme threat that is unanticipated, unpredicted, or uncontrolled. Noradrenaline serves to rigidify—i.e., "freeze frame"—the perception and memory of the threat and extinguish alternative perceptions and memories (for example, the occurrence of flashbacks). The shocked emotion occurs in the instinctive survival responses of the brain, which are not under conscious control of the officer. Neurological activity occurring in the "fight or flight" area of the brain is fueled in part by the hormone norepinephrine or noradrenaline, which mobilizes the body for emergency reaction, prolongs the perception and memory of the shocking event, and inhibits the perception or memory of any other circumstance.

The perceptual shock impact of norepinephrine in a police officer can be seen in instances where officer reports are not corroborated by the physical evidence found at the scene. At the moment of unanticipated, unpredicted, or an uncontrollable and extreme threat, the effects of norepinephrine lead to a "freeze framing" of the perception of that moment in time. Thereafter, the level of threat may actually be diminished, but the lessening of the threat does not register in the officer's conscious mind. Officers tend then to report a level of threat, or justify the use of lethal force they applied, that may have existed at point "a," but did not at point "b," when the officer actually responded.

Unnecessary Losses
A number of years ago, a police officer was fired from his department following investigation and hearings into an officer-involved shooting he had been involved in. He was a good-hearted and honest young man and reported his actions in this incident exactly as he recalled them. The physical evidence at the scene, however, did not corroborate his report.

The officer reported that he had followed a vehicle that matched the description of a grand larceny auto until the car rolled through a stop sign without stopping. This provided the officer with a reason to pull the vehicle over. However, as the officer lit up his overhead lights, the suspect vehicle took off at high speed in an apparent attempt to evade apprehension. The officer transmitted his information and location and reported that a possible grand larceny suspect was fleeing.

The vehicle pursuit became a foot pursuit when the suspect had a traffic collision. The suspect fled through the backyards of a townhouse complex. An approximately six-foot-tall wooden fence bordered each of the backyards. The suspect began to vault the fences from yard to yard, trying to run from the officer.

The officer followed the suspect over the fences and from yard to yard, trying to close the distance between himself and the fleeing suspect. The officer's expectations were similar to those normally held by officers who pursue suspects on foot: "I've got to get as close to him as I can. He's trying to get away from me. My job is to catch him. He will not get away from me....I don't give up." The officer believed the suspect would continue to try to escape, and that he, the officer, would try to close the distance between himself and the suspect as the latter tried to vault the next fence.

At one fence, however, the suspect did something totally unexpected to the officer. He was poised to vault a fence with his arms up as if to grab hold of the top of the fence when, suddenly, he halted his movements and abruptly changed his behavior. His back facing the officer, the suspect dropped his hands in front of him and went to the front of his pants at his waistband. The officer thought the suspect was attempting to extract something from his pants, but the suspect's body prevented the officer from seeing clearly what the suspect was doing. The suspect now dropped into a crouch and began to turn aggressively toward the officer.

The officer thought: "He has a gun...he's going for a gun....If I let him turn, he will shoot me." The officer's perception of a lethal threat was sufficient to cause him to fear for his life and he decided to use lethal force since he could not give the suspect the opportunity to turn and get off a shot before he did. Trying to stop the suspect from turning, the officer aimed at the man's lower left back and fired.

The suspect turned back to face the fence, placed his hands on top of it, and pulled himself up and over the fence to continue his flight. The officer was dumbfounded: "How could I have missed?" the officer thought. "I'm a good marksman. I was *this* close to the suspect. I know I must have missed him. How could he continue to flee unless I missed?"

But the officer had not missed the suspect. The suspect collapsed and died after running about forty feet. However, the entry wound was not in the suspect's lower back but in his stomach. There were wood fragments from the fence in the entry wound. In the officer's mind, he had fired into the suspect's back before the suspect had jumped over the fence. In reality, however, the officer hadn't fired until the suspect was hanging over the other side of the fence.

Naturally, the officer reported the incident the way he had seen it and wouldn't change his statement. At the time of the shooting he thought he was going to die. He indicated that he had made the decision to shoot the suspect in the back to prevent the latter from turning and getting "the drop on me." He said he had seen himself shoot the suspect in the back.

No one who investigated the incident, no one who defended the officer from the association attorney's office, and no one on the panel of commissioners that decided his fate had a clue about perceptual shock reactions and the chemical basis for perceptual trauma in police officers during unanticipated events containing a lethal threat. The officer could not explain why he reported that he shot the suspect before the latter vaulted the fence, when it was apparent to all that he had not actually shot until the suspect was on the other side.

It was a very sad situation. The officer was fired for shooting "out of policy." He lost his job and his home, because he could no longer pay for it. No one thought he was lying; indeed, he had always been known for his honesty. It was just out of policy to shoot someone through a fence.

It does not take much imagination to accept that an individual can well have perceptual shock when he or she faces death.

The public expects police officers not to have logical human perceptual trauma when they face a lethal threat, but officers do. Problems occur when the officers have no idea that their senses are "playing tricks" on them.

Recall, if you will, the story of the officer who was ambushed by the would-be rapist in the beauty salon. The officer had no idea he was about to be in a gunfight to save his life and the lives of innocent women and children. He had participated in simulation training in which he had been ambushed during a scenario where he had to respond to an unanticipated threat while his weapon was holstered. He had had to engage the actor in the simulation until he was consistently victorious.

In the training, the officer's brain had begun to experience fewer and fewer shock or surprise reactions as the scenarios progressed. He had begun to feel less reactive and more proactive as he became familiar with the act of responding to an unanticipated, unpredictable, but extreme threat. He had begun to feel in control when faced with such a situation.

Consequently, the officer after the event was able to describe with complete accuracy the rapid and immediate response he was able to perform. The officer presented in the example above, however, had not been trained in the recognition and management of perceptual trauma in law enforcement stress and had as a result suffered the loss of all he had worked for when his report was not corroborated by physical evidence.

If an officer has previously trained and practiced tools and techniques for minimizing the impact of flashbacks and other post-traumatic stress reactions, he or she will rapidly regain control over the physical, emotional, mental, and behavioral aspects of his or her life. Indeed, the officer is likely to become stronger for the experience of personal control he or she has exerted over a traumatic event. If not, one in three officers is likely to develop severe post-incident stress reactions that could permanently damage his or her health, relationships with loved ones, work, and life.

Most people believe that the impacts from post-traumatic stress will show themselves in emotional and visual after-effects. Such is not the case for police officers. By the time they are on the job for six to eight years, police officers have likely developed effective coping mechanisms for management of emotional distress. They have, unfortunately, no such coping mechanisms for the physical after-effects of trauma such as hypertension, chronic gastrointestinal damage, or physical pain caused by their untrained reactions to single-episode stress.

The second issue raised here deals with the impact of perceptual trauma upon police officer decision-making, the use of tactics, and the ability of officers to justify why they did what they did during tactical encounters. Perceptual trauma will likely intrude upon or interrupt officers' ability to analyze and make decisions during developing or rapidly changing events. Perceptual trauma is prevented by acts of pre-planned, purposeful, or conscious concentration on the tasks required for personal control.

The part of the brain that becomes active when officers concentrate is that part that registers changes in circumstances—threats—and the need to alter any intended tactics.

The chemical and electrical and hormonal changes in the brain that have previously resulted in officer shock or perceptual trauma can be controlled to a great extent by the development of officer habit patterns—i.e., constant practice of specific behaviors, thoughts, and emotions that create personal control and victory.

1. See, for example, Violanti *et al.*, 1986, for a study on life expectancy of police officers.
2. United States of America Bureau of Census, 1998.
3. Violanti *et al.*, 1986.
4. Cannon, 1953.
5. Brod, 1959, 1971; Froberg, Karlsson, Levi, & Lidberg, 1971; Henry & Stephens, 1977; Ametz, Fjellner, Eneroth, & Kallner, 1986; Axelrod & Reisine, 1984; McCabe & Schneiderman, 1984.
6. Researchers describe this condition as "the state typical of daily hassles, that of striving to gain and maintain control." See Frankenhaeuser, 1986, p. 107; Lundberg & Frankenhaeuser, 1980.
7. Seligman, 1975.
8. Lundberg & Forsman, 1979.
9. Frankenhaeuser, Lundberg, & Forsman, 1980; Johansson & Sanden, 1982; Urwin, Baade, and Levine, 1978.
10. Bandura, 1977, 1982a, 1982b; Thompson, 1981; Krantz, 1980; Seligman, 1975; Averill, 1973.
11. Frankenhaeuser, 1981.
12. Karasek, 1979; Theorell, Lind, Lundberg, Christensson, & Edhag, 1981.
13. Blum, 1994, 1998.
14. Violanti *et al.*, 1986; Fell, Richard, & Wallace, 1980.
15. Blum, 1998.

16. The Random House Dictionary, 1980.
17. DSM-III-R, American Psychiatric Association, 1987.
18. Ibid.
19. Ibid.
20. Ibid.
21. Pitman, 1989, p. 222.

7: *Mental Conditioning: Training Methods for Maintaining the Will to Survive*

Perception is all-important in training methods for the will to survive. Individuals' perceptions of things are what determine their entire sense of reality. Police officers' perceptions determine what reactions their body will go through and what their behavioral response will be under conditions of grave threat or danger. The actual circumstance that an officer encounters actually exerts a much smaller influence upon him or her than how he or she perceives the threat or danger.[1]

Perception determines what visual meaning and mental assessment will be made about the nature of the circumstance the police officer is encountering. Perception determines the officer's appraisal of his or her ability to overcome that threat. At the moment of threat, the officer's brain undergoes some specific type of activity, either to dominate the suspect by physical action or to withdraw from the threat. It is easy for police officers to say they will not be defeated. How the officers actually pull off the unwavering determination to be victorious, however, should no longer be up to fate or circumstance. Training in mental conditioning and pre-programming for mastery provide the tools an officer can use to increase the strength and stamina of the will to survive after the officer has been shot, stabbed, or bludgeoned.

As we have seen, police training at the firing range or anywhere else involves the repetition of sequences or patterns of an action in order for a skill to be learned. Such training for a specific skill has a counterpart in psychology called **response patterning**. Response patterning refers to the manner in which a behavior is formed, learned, or conditioned.

When you first learn a new skill, you do it by conscious or purposeful acts. You have to be conscious of the sequence of actions you must take because there has not yet been response patterning to make the behavior automatic for you. As you become more skilled, however, you become less conscious of what you are doing and simply do it. Patterning, then, refers to the learning and conditioning of a planned sequence of behavior that is done automatically and continuously under the conditions for which the behavior was developed. Again, you don't have to be consciously aware of the sequence of actions. You have simply learned to do it.

Training Methods for Developing and Maintaining the Will to Survive

Training for the will to survive involves the programming of two types of conditioned-behavior patterns in police officers: mental conditioning and physical conditioning.

Mental Conditioning

This refers to activities designed to condition the brain to countermand the normal human tendency toward "freezing" during an encounter with momentarily overwhelming circumstances or experiences of defeat.

It is only when the brain encounters circumstances that it perceives as overwhelming will it use cortisol to quiet, lessen, weaken, or "freeze" the body's combat to protect itself from exertion it feels it cannot afford to expend anymore. During the time, however, an individual is engaged in mental activity that generates the perception of mastery, the individual's body will not decrease or weaken its levels of energy when faced with a threat. The brain is much more likely to increase energy levels when it perceives personal control—i.e., mastery—in the individual's response to the threat.

Therefore, training the officer in the kind of mental activity that triggers and maintains mastery activities will increase energic levels—in the brain and body—and subsequently decrease any likelihood of a weakening response in the officer's perception, such as the experience of defeat. Pre-programming this mental activity under conditions of potential or imminent injury will minimize the likelihood of a shock reaction being created in the officer's brain when he or she experiences being shot, stabbed, or struck. Such shock reaction occurring at the moment the officers perceive themselves to be wounded could well extinguish their will to survive.

In his excellent book *Peak Performance*, Garfield presents several studies that document the performance of a group of world-class athletes who were trained to perform mental rehearsal of *each of the movements* of their event as well as their physical training, as an integral part of their training and preparation. Another group of athletes at the same level of talent performed the same physical part of their training as the other group did, but did not perform disciplined mental rehearsal. The first group did noticeably better.

Mental rehearsal of each of the movements substantially improves the performance a person is able to achieve in an intentionally performed task.[2] In training, the neuromuscular processes that the officer's brain goes through in making connections with the muscles the officer uses to fight for his or her life are first performed in the absence of the threat. Then, when the actual threat is encountered, the neuromuscular processes that have been conditioned by practice will activate the officer's fight for his or her life without conscious deliberation.[3] This is important, since, with conscious deliberation, there is always the danger that the officer's response to a lethal threat will be delayed, particularly if the officer feels he or she might be defeated.

But—and this is most important—there has to be movement and motion involved when the officer is being trained in visually rehearsing the situation. In other words, the increase in performance can only be achieved through the officer visualizing him- or herself *causing movement and the changes to the encountered circumstance caused by the movement.*[4] This need is especially acute because individuals just starting out in training their mental habits have a tendency to report scenes they see statically: "If this circumstance occurs, this is what I will do then." The individuals are, as it were, taking still pictures with their mind's eye. They perceive the scene or circumstance with a tendency to freeze the mental image. This is what is meant by "freeze frame" in perception, referring to an abrupt stopping of the circumstance that is being observed. *Officers need to see themselves moving, changing the conditions of the scene with their actions, and then "watching" the conditions change as a direct result of the actions they took.*

Unestahl's research[5] has demonstrated that athletes' use of mental rehearsal using static or still images "subconsciously directed their bodies to remain set in particular positions—even when performing complex actions that required constant change in response to changing circumstance." If an officer is shot, stabbed, or bludgeoned, remaining "set in particular positions" will cost the officer his or her life. This technique should not be mistaken for those that reduce stress through visual imagery (attempting to defuse arousal via a pleasant vision that relaxes the person). Visual imagery as a stress-reduction technique is quite helpful in extinguishing flashbacks of previously encountered traumatic incidents. The kind of mental rehearsal for police officers discussed here is intended to instill very specific patterns of automatic, highly aggressive responses to a grave threat in individuals who may not have had such behavioral rehearsal before.

This doesn't mean that new applicants cannot perform properly and bravely in response to a threat. It just means they need to spend a good deal of disciplined time practicing a mental rehearsal of behaviors—behaviors that create a shift in the situation the officer is encountering if the officer is successfully attacked by a felon. The officer's thoughts are then likely to be as follows: "I knew this is what I would feel like. I was prepared to conquer this pain and fear. I have been victorious over and over in my vision and I will be victorious now. Now I move from the victim role to the aggressor. Instead of the surprise or shock of being struck stopping me, or my pain stopping me, it mobilizes me to action."

Using the Mind's Eye to Rehearse the Will to Survive

Learning how to use imagery

The first step in mental rehearsal is to practice becoming skilled at creating images that one sees in the mind's eye. It is a mistake for officers to assume that all they have to do is use their imaginations. Mental rehearsal is a skill that must be learned and practiced like any other skill for which excellence or peak performance is sought.

The first thing to do when beginning any visualization is to relax. When we relax, blood flow increases, energizing the brain's visual cortex, where mental imagery occurs.

The officer should recall an event he or she experienced that was particularly dramatic—some event that struck him or her because of his or her feelings for it. The officer should try to recall the event's smell and colors, how the air felt upon the skin, and the sounds he or she heard. Officers should attempt to remember what they thought or felt during the event.

The officer should then take a deep breath, inhale to a count of four, hold for four, then exhale completely and fully while counting to four. Officers should slow and deepen their breathing rate to increase the clarity of the images. They should focus their attention on as many details as possible in the visualized image.

After the image is clear in their mind's eye, officers should erase the image from their mind.[6] Garfield recommends doing this by looking toward an artificial light *with eyes closed*. Officers should create a blank or neutral space in their minds, like a television screen with no picture showing. After about twenty seconds of focusing on a blank space, they should recall the image previously created. The degree of practice and control achieved in recalling clear, vivid images will determine the ultimate success of officers in using mental rehearsal.[7]

The final preparatory phase in using the mind's eye to rehearse the will to survive is practicing the visualization of the officer's best past performance. When an officer has been shot, stabbed, or bludgeoned, his or her will to survive and physical survival will require the maximum possible acts of will and strength. Research has shown that recalling a past activity or event in which the individual has performed at the peak of his or her performance will best prepare the individual to create a mental rehearsal that maximizes effort.

Again, according to Unestahl,[8] the lessons of research of peak performance in athletic events are that, regardless of the competitive outcome, "the significant event is a period of time that...provided an experience of actualization that corresponds to...peak perform-ance...." Peak performance is achieved by high-intensity goal-directed behavior (exerting the will to win) and mind-body integration (doing the tasks that impose one's will upon a circumstance).

Procedure for Mental Rehearsal of the Will to Survive

Step One

To create the most realistic or vivid imagery to use in mental rehearsal, use one of the relaxation techniques available in any book on stress reduction in order to achieve deep relaxation prior to starting any visualization activity.

Step Two

The officer should envision the most important things in his or her world. Is it a loved one? A goal? Things the officer has perhaps wanted to do and hasn't done yet? Officers should envision what is ahead of them. They should attempt to imagine how they would stop a felon from raping their child or spouse or mother. They should ask themselves what they would do in that circumstance. They should honestly examine what they would do to save the most precious thing in their lives if they were being attacked.[9]

I have been asked on a number of occasions to assist detectives about to interview or interrogate a suspect by providing a psychological profile of that individual's character patterns, and have seen the harm done to the victims by those suspects. I know that you cannot take anything back once it happens. You can only prevent its occurrence. These experiences have reinforced my knowledge that with my last and dying breath, I will do anything and everything necessary to save my wife and children from harm.

Make a decision

Officers need to decide how much they are willing to call upon within themselves to fight to save their lives. Once they make this decision, they should envision themselves doing the things they would do to save their loved ones from attack. They should envision the change in circumstances they create when they vanquish the dangerous felon and save (for example) their family. They should see themselves hugging and being hugged by those they've saved. They should see what it took to accomplish this act: What does it make them feel to have to do this? They should acknowledge what that feeling is. No one is asking them to enjoy visualizing violence. They should just be the victor and not the victim.

Step Three

Officers should create an image of a situation in which they are responding to various calls of unknown trouble—say a man with a gun, a silent alarm, shots fired, a mentally ill person threatening others, etc. Officers should visualize themselves driving or walking to the scene. They should take the time to make a conscious motion picture of what each of their senses experiences. Officers should ask themselves: "What am I thinking about? What kind of mood am I in? What sounds do I hear?" Officers should create a motion picture of themselves, perhaps, in a darkened, unpleasant area, where it smells bad. They should imagine they are announcing themselves as a police officer. They can't see well. They feel alert but uneasy.

Step Four

Officers should visualize a suspect ambushing them. They should feel the shock and surprise and initial fear. They should ask themselves: "What sounds am I hearing? What do I see?" Officers should pay particular attention to details of the image of the suspect and his weapon: "He's got a gun. I see muzzle flash....I've been shot. What an impact! I am vulnerable. I've been stabbed. It hurts. I expected a totally different circumstance!"

Officers should visualize what it feels like at the moment they are vulnerable. Again, officers *must* visualize what is happening in the form of movement. Then they should visualize what it feels now they've been struck. Do they feel harmed? Are they afraid? What do they see? What does it feel like to be shot, stabbed, or bludgeoned? Do they feel weakened? Do they think they're going to die? Does it make them angry? What are they thinking?

It is *essential* that officers go through minute details of their vision. The more detail they obtain in the visualization, the more likely their nerves and muscles will be actually rehearsing what they will do if such an event occurs. Officers need to realize that if they remain feeling helpless they will die.

What officers need to do after Step Four is, I admit, controversial. The reader will recall that in an earlier chapter I suggested that feelings of rage, terror, or other extreme survival-oriented emotional states were triggers for the release of norepinephrine, the body's fuel for emergency arousal.

Persons concerned with liability may balk at the thought of police officers practicing or rehearsing rage and hatred towards suspects. They may raise concerns that such rehearsal may predispose officers to becoming angrier or more aggressive in circumstances that do not justify such responses. In actuality, the vast majority of police officers use a tremendous and continuous amount of restraint when dealing with resistive subjects. Today they may well have increased the potential risk to themselves because of the concern most officers feel about being punished for performing the less attractive—but most dangerous—parts of police work.

The concerns that many risk-management personnel have expressed about survival-oriented mental training is, in my opinion, misplaced. When police officers are properly trained in mastery-oriented mental and tactical control techniques, they will be more successful at controlling the scene and involved subjects with less severe levels of control and/or force. This is so because they will intervene in a decisive and rapid manner, gaining the initiative and taking control at lower levels of threatening suspect behavior.

Over the past twenty years, I have come to the conclusion that having citizens feel closer to police officers and trusting them more does not require us to destroy police officers' aggressiveness. I believe that the best way to protect against excessive or improper police action is to create excellence in police officers. Training excellence is achieved only when the elements of practice are most similar to the actual behaviors that officers encounter in the field.

Police agencies throughout the country have, for at least the past eight years, been attempting to become more client-centered, i.e., to develop a more service-oriented approach to police work. Police officers are to be problem solvers for the community's quality of life—in addition to the community's need for purely law enforcement police activities. Great effort has been made to demonstrate to interested community members that the police are responsive to their needs. Attorneys have begun a previously unheard of monetary assault upon municipal, county, state, and federal coffers by lawsuits alleging officers' abuse of police authority through excessive use of force. Court decisions have been rendered that have lessened the types and amounts of physical control measures officers can legally use in defense of themselves or others.

At the same time, police agencies have purchased training programs in large numbers to provide officers with verbal control techniques which the agencies' leadership expect will lessen the severity or need for officers' use of force. Aggressive actions in the field taken by officers have been scrutinized and investigated, and very often officers have been subjected to discipline.

The message is clear. Aggression with subjects and suspects is not a good thing for police officers to use in the field. The problem I have with a logic that sees the solution to excessive force in an extinction of police aggression is that it may well be that extinguishing officer aggression is more likely to result in officers needing to use *greater degrees of force*. Officers' hesitancy to engage in decisive, initiative-seizing actions very often permits the severity of the situation to escalate to a point where greater levels of force are required. Suspects are much more likely to gain a position of advantage over officers when, for example, they continue to engage in verbal commands *even when the suspect is in the act of attempting to murder them!*[10]

I am in no way advocating a lessening of community-based and problem-oriented policing. Such methods of policing greatly benefit the communities served. Nor am I criticizing the use of verbal resources to control a situation. What I am advocating is a reality check in the training and conditioning of police officers. Dangerous and vicious criminals continue to prey upon the weak and innocent. Police officers must be as prepared and supported (by their agencies) to engage in life or death struggle just as much as they are to help communities increase the quality of life therein.

There must never be an "acceptable" casualty rate for police officers, such as that discussed in military operations (the amount of losses beyond which a fighting force is no longer viable in combat). And yet the general support for a cessation of aggressive action cannot help but compromise officers' safety in potentially dangerous field encounters. Police officers continue to be murdered. And I continue to have the painful honor to sit with the survivors of murdered police officers at memorials honoring their memory.

Aggression is not brutality. It is a forceful, explosive action performed for the purpose of seizing the initiative in potentially dangerous circumstances. Aggression is an approach to life that exists in order to achieve mastery and personal control in an individual's life activities. And sometimes, aggression includes the use of physical controls that are immediately and decisively applied to resistive subjects in order to prevent escalation in the levels of threat the officer will encounter.

The term "excessive" when applied to uses of force implies that an officer has used a greater severity of physical control than was required or made necessary by a suspect's actions. The term "improper" when applied to uses of force implies that an officer has used physical force in a manner that misuses the authority given by law to police officers. The term "excellence" when applied to uses of force implies that the officer has engaged in an accurate assessment of the conditions of the scene that she or he encounters. "Excellence" suggests that the officer has correctly understood the suspect's reactions to his or her presence, and has appraised the likely conditions he or she will need to manage and how capable he or she is of managing those conditions—a performance of tactics designed to gain and maintain the initiative in subject encounters that generates mastery by the officer according to policy, law, and ethical values. Aggression—at all levels of force, including verbal methods— in this sense is the tool with which the officer safely and properly accomplishes the tasks required to "protect and serve."

I have seen a growing tendency for officers to hesitate before becoming aggressive and containing possibly escalating subjects or suspects at that moment—and thus allowing situations to continue to the point where greater levels of force are required. This may be because the officer feared being punished or criticized, or because he or she felt they lacked experience in coping with the threat that now is life-threatening. There is thus all the more reason to consistently practice mental rehearsal for the will to survive.

Step Five

As soon as officers realize that, if they remain vulnerable or feel hopeless, they will die, they should watch themselves fill up and explode with rage and hatred. They should become aware that their pain is no barometer of how badly they're hurt. As the police officer said when she was shot in the chest in the ambush in her driveway, "Think about the pain later...now it's time to fight."

Officers should visualize being extremely violent against the felon. They should listen and hear the sounds of mortal combat. They should give it everything they have and more.

They should recognize that they tried to tell the suspect to stop, put the weapon down, and that the suspect was told the violence didn't have to happen. However, they should acknowledge that there is a moment when the police officer has to realize that the suspect will not stop. The officer should visualize the moment when only one of them will live, and the officer must ensure that the person left standing is the officer and not the suspect.

Officers should imagine what it feels like to be filled with hatred for what the suspect would take from them; they should allow the hate they feel at that life being taken away fuel their reaction. Officers should watch as they overcome the suspect, feel him weakening, and feel their own confidence building as they see themselves win. They should see themselves walk into the arms of the loved ones they visualized in Step Two. Officers continue to have a life with them because they did what they did.

Officers should concentrate on visualizing the victory, not the fatigue they feel. There is a quotation made by Vince Lombardi, the late and great coach of the feared Green Bay Packers. To summarize, he noted that the moment that most defines an individual and all he or she could aspire to or represent—the ultimate statement about their life—comes at the moment when they are lying drained, spent, after giving all that they were on the field of combat...victorious. Visualize yourself living this. Remember: What the mind can conceive the body can achieve.

In order to encourage the idea of motion, officers should have created a motion picture of which they are the director. They are also the lead actor in the movie. They should fill in the cast of characters and give them their parts. They make the movie and define the ending.[11]

No officer can ever predict when he or she will be ambushed or attacked. It doesn't matter where the officer works, how busy his or her jurisdiction is, or what time of the day it is. If, however, the officer has done the work of mental rehearsal, his or her brain will have developed conditioned neural pathways that have performed the actions visualized and practiced. When the officer faces the actual threat, he or she will find it unnecessary to perform conscious deliberation about how to maintain the will to survive in the face of apparent defeat. In a potentially lethal encounter, officers face a simple choice. They will either perform at the peak of mental clarity, tactical ability, and physical aggression...or they will die.

Physical Conditioning

I do not presume to be an expert in the field of weaponless defense or armed defense. However, I have studied how people win and lose in order to determine what types of training increase strength and stamina. In working with police officers who have been physically assaulted, I have asked them about what regimens of physical conditioning—or the lack thereof—they had been consistently engaged in subsequent to the assault.

Some of the officers' injuries had resulted in decreases in their vigor and ability to maintain effective physical defenses. Others had incurred severe injury through being hit on the head but had overcome the suspect who had ambushed them. What became evident to me was that the officers who were most successful in withstanding and then conquering an attempt upon their life were those who consistently trained to condition their body to countermand the tiring, weakening, slowing, or quieting effect of cortisol.

When we exert ourselves, the brain appraises the load being placed upon muscles and connective tissue and assesses the individual's ability to manage it. If the brain perceives that the load is too great for the individual to manage without incurring injury, a defensive adaptation occurs in which cortisol deflates muscle-skeletal activity to protect itself. As readers will remember, the body's overall defensive adaptation (in which the body's intensity levels and activity are decreased) is called conservation withdrawal.

When an officer is in hand-to-hand combat with a suspect, he or she has a simple option about how to respond to the suspect's attempt to take his or her weapon and/or kill the officer. The officer has to respond to the threat with appropriate levels of physical intensity and duration of effort or she or he will die. The officer must countermand any experience of fatigue with increased vigor. And he or she must countermand any feeling of pain or physical distress with increased intensity.

When an officer has been wounded or injured, the form of physical conditioning that appears to be most successful at countermanding any weakening effects of cortisol released in reaction to the wound involves prolonged, gradual *increasing of the intensity of effort over time.*

The specific type of exercise the officer performs is unimportant for this countermanding effect. What is important is that the officer conditions his or her body over a long period of time and slowly but steadily increases the intensity of effort. To avoid over-training, it is suggested that officers begin this regimen at sixty-five percent of their maximal intensity of effort. This level of intensity is performed for five training sessions. Repetitions or volume are increased across the five training sessions, while maintaining this level of intensity. On the sixth training session, the intensity of effort should be increased by five percent. This intensity is performed for five training sessions. Repetitions or volume are increased across the five training sessions while maintaining sixty-five percent intensity.

The intensity of level of effort is increased every fifth training session, and each training session has slight increases in intensity as well. After reaching ninety-percent intensity, it is suggested that the individual rest one week, set a new height of 100-percent maximum intensity of effort, and then begin at sixty-five percent of this new number for five sessions, etc. Officers are urged to limit the amount of work they engage in that is over ninety-percent intensity, because the neuromuscular system deteriorates after three to four weeks of workload intensity above ninety percent. If officers desire to maintain such a high intensity of effort, they should be changing the exercise they engage in every two to three weeks in order to avoid over-training difficulties.

As the intensity of effort increases, the officer will experience fatigue, discomfort, or pain. Once more, the officer is faced with a simple option: Either he or she breaks the impasse with a greater vigor and intensity or conditions him- or herself to allow fatigue, discomfort, or pain to defeat them.

What happens over the course of several training sessions is that the neuromuscular activities that overcome all the adversity encountered during intense physical effort are conditioned in the officer's brain to form a habit. The brain now becomes familiar with increasing the body's effort and intensity of physical activity in the presence of fatigue or distress.

If an officer is injured or wounded during an assault, his or her brain will then be highly likely to increase their intensity of effort during combat without the need of conscious deliberation. Thus, when the going gets tougher, the body only gets stronger. In such situations, therefore, cortisol is likely to *increase* energic levels in the presence of injury instead of manifesting its protective tendency to decrease or shut down exertion in order to conserve the body.

By integrating into officer training efforts physical and mental conditioning programs for mastery and victory, officers will more likely be able to maintain the will to survive when they have been shot, stabbed, or bludgeoned—irrespective of individual abilities and tendencies. If these programs are not followed, it is up to chance or circumstance as to which officer lives and which dies. There are obviously many different types of training regimens that enhance physical conditioning in police officers. However, adding a program where intensity of effort is increased on a continuing and prolonged basis will equalize to a great extent the ability of police officers to survive lethal assault.

---

1. See, for example, Girdano and Everly (1986); Ellis, 1973; Lazarus, 1966a, 1966b; Lazarus & Folkman, 1984; Meichenbaum, 1977; Meichenbaum & Jaremko, 1983.
2. Garfield, 1984.
3. Ibid.
4. Unestahl, 1979.
5. Unestahl, 1976.
6. Garfield, 1984.
7. Ibid.
8. Unestahl, 1976.
9. My wife has long believed that such thoughts as this—which I have spent a lifetime engaging in—were signs of a *paranoid* person. However, paranoia refers to an unwarranted tendency to perceive threat or harm. I have always believed, from the time I was first allowed into the playground at school and saw that a person could get his or her butt kicked there, that you never knew what precaution saved you. You should use as many as you can.
10. LEOKA Study, 1994.
11. Garfield, 1984.

8: Stress Management Resources for Officer Wellness

As I mentioned earlier in this book, the traditional method that police officers use to cope with distressed or disturbed perception or emotion is roughly as follows: "If I don't think about it, it won't bother me. If it doesn't bother me, I don't have a problem with it. If I don't have a problem with it, I'm *okfine*." As we have seen, there are obviously very good reasons why officers are trained and socialized to avoid conscious awareness or disclosure of distressed or disturbed emotions.

However, as I hope I have made very clear throughout this book, if an officer does not command and control his or her mental, emotional, and physical responses to episodes that elicit intense psychological and physical reactions, those episodes will exert a greater impact upon the officer. To summarize: When encounters in the field precipitate emotions that a police officer is not in control of, the uncontrolled intrusion of those conditions is likely to impede his or her ability to use their training effectively as well as to respond strategically to the threat.

It is because dealing with stress effectively makes police officers better officers that managing stress should not be perceived as merely "making the officer happy" or "feel better" about his or her work.

Stress management serves to develop specific response patterns in police officers that have proven effective in lessening the probability of errors in strategic thinking and/or defeat in officers' attempts to command and control encounters in the field. By neutralizing or suspending the harmful impact of intrusive or uncontrolled conditions, officers improve their ability to maintain control of their thoughts, emotions, and physical reactions or behavior.

We have seen how external situations—such as family or domestic conflicts they feel uncertain about how to fix, or scrutiny from the department—can distract officers. Such preoccupation compromises officer safety because it intrudes upon and impairs accurate perception and strategic thinking in the field.

Stress Management Technology

It is worth summarizing the techniques that have proven successful in enhancing police officers' self-control. They have five component parts, each of which must be utilized for effective symptom extinction:

1. Identification of trigger stimuli
2. Defusing the psychophysiological hyperarousal reaction when triggers occur
3. Application of balance behaviors to countermand the harmful impact of triggers
4. Relaxation and visualization techniques to counteract post-traumatic reactions
5. Action plan for wellness

1. Identification of Trigger Stimuli

There are characteristics or ingredients active in stressful encounters that precipitate stress reactions in police officers. The first step in managing police stress is for the officer to identify what reactions they experience under conditions of stress.

These reactions may be as follows: gastrointestinal symptoms, headache pain, shortness of breath, chest pain, back or neck pain, sleep disturbances, withdrawal from normally enjoyed activities, irritability or impatience with loved ones, lapses in concentration and memory, or difficulties in calming oneself once one is aroused.

If the officer is experiencing these symptoms, he or she should first list or recall each time at work when a particular stress reaction was experienced.

The next step is to identify the characteristics or ingredients that existed in those incidents. In other words, the officer may recall: "There was nothing I could do; the harm was already done; I felt helpless; there were insufficient resources; I knew the parents were guilty and felt such anger and dismay; there were unknown circumstances; I kept remembering the smells; I couldn't save my partner; I was made to feel like a defendant; I kept seeing the look in the child's eyes; I felt the child's pain, etc."

These characteristics, active at the moments of impact upon the police officer, are **trigger stimuli**. Every time and any time they are experienced, they trigger a stress reaction in the individual.

I have recommended that police officers become proficient in recognizing trigger stimuli. Officers then can apply tools and techniques to control their arousal levels *whenever trigger stimuli are encountered.* Officers who have developed these techniques report a substantial decrease in symptom severity and frequency and the duration of distressing and disturbing stress reactions when they are faced by trigger stimuli in encounters.

Not training police officers in stress control has contributed to the high levels of psychophysiological symptoms currently documented in police officers. We expect our police to take care of their equipment; likewise, police agencies should be ensuring that an officer is as well conditioned and in as good a shape as the equipment he or she uses.

It should be noted here that all ranks of police officers have reported identical levels of psychophysiological stress symptoms. Therefore, techniques to identify trigger stimuli and manage the hyperarousal response should be an organizational effort rather than focused solely on one or more ranks or classification of employee.

2. Defusing the Psychophysiological Hyperarousal Reaction

Breathing Techniques
Breathing properly is essential for enhanced mental and physical health in police personnel. Shallow, rapid breathing—the pattern that occurs most often when an officer is under conditions of stress—is a corollary of anxiety states, depression, and fatigue. *Proper breathing is an antidote to stress!* The extensive benefits of proper breathing techniques will be observed after several weeks of *continued practice*.

Breathing properly has been shown to assist the proper use of service weapons. However, rarely has effective training in effective breathing been used as a method to control, defuse, and manage the hyperarousal reaction. I recommend the following techniques for personal control:

Deep breathing. Developing the *habit* of deep breathing will help to defuse or recondition the hyperarousal reaction and allow the individual to defuse tension and stress levels. Although this technique may appear unusual or too "touchy-feely" for police officers, slowing and deepening breathing will control and modulate the alarm reaction that is habitually maintained in police officers.

Natural breathing. During periods of tension and stress, an officer can, if he or she focuses upon breathing, notice sighs or yawns. These are generally a sign that the individual is not getting enough oxygen. When done properly, natural breathing releases tension and can be done at will to control psychophysiological arousal. This technique is based upon yoga exercises and permits the individual using it to control the body's arousal levels under conditions of tension or stress. The inhalation begins at the diaphragm rather than the chest. This is done because skeletal muscles around the chest are tense and restrictive under conditions of stress.

After first inhaling at the diaphragm, the officer should inflate the stomach and then the chest. He or she should breathe in for a count of four, hold the breath for four when the trunk is completely inflated, then exhale to deflation over four counts.

3. Balancing Behaviors to Countermand Triggers

Balancing behaviors are planned, strategic activities designed to countermand the harmful impact of trigger stimuli. There are three primary balance behavior strategies:

Physical Conditioning

One of the most important and positive effects of physical conditioning is its impact upon mood states and emotions. Different types of physical-conditioning activity have been shown to create predictable effects upon officers' emotional conditions, mood states, and energy levels.

High-intensity exercise can be used when the individual's reactions to stress tend to result in depressive reactions—i.e., feeling a lack of vital energy, withdrawing from normally enjoyed activities, being despondent emotionally, feeling fatigued even after rest, feeling helpless or hopeless. As we saw in the last chapter, high-intensity exercise refers to the application of intensity of effort from approximately sixty to ninety percent of one's maximal intensity, with a gradual increase in intensity of the exercise over time.

Therefore, if the individual is a walker, and walks one mile per exercise period, then next week the walk would be increased to either one and one-quarter mile, or the intensity of walking be increased so that less time is used to walk the same distance. High-intensity exercise increases the body's discharge of hormones that promote positive aggression. These hormones and the associated positive aggression exert a surprisingly effective dampening effect upon depression of mood and emotion. This exercise causes an increase in the availability of serotonin in the brain. Serotonin levels determine mood and emotional states by dampening the parts of the brain that create emotional upset. If a person has too little serotonin he or she is depressed; too much and the person is anxious. During periods of depressed mood, high-intensity exercise should be applied in relatively short exercise periods, with "bursts" of activity.

Low-intensity exercise is used when the individual's reaction to stress tends to result in "antsy," agitated, or anxious reactions, leading to difficulty relaxing, disturbances in sleep, rapid or shallow breathing, feelings of uneasiness, or premonitions of harm or threat. Low-intensity exercise develops aerobic conditioning and is applied at intensities from forty to sixty percent of maximal intensity of effort for a longer period of exercise.

Low-intensity exercise does not generally increase the intensity of effort so much as it increases the duration of effort. Low-intensity exercise increases the body's discharge of natural painkillers, or endorphins, which greatly assist in defusing the hyperarousal reaction and lessen the impact of adrenaline toxicity.

Hobbies

As simple as it might seem, a hobby is of great importance in managing the hyperarousal response. Most police officers enjoyed hobbies in the past, but stopped them when they began to work in law enforcement. Hobbies are of great benefit in reconditioning the brain's tendency to activate the alarm (neuroendocrine reaction) as well as lowering the individual's tension levels (unless individuals use their hobbies to become irritable, angry, frustrated, or disappointed in themselves).

It is never too late to take up a hobby. Later is too late! None of us should postpone the time when we most enjoy our life.

Improve Your Relationship

One of the most immediate and telling impacts of police work stress—and in persons who experience depression—is the withdrawal from potentially (or previously) enjoyable activities or involvement with people. The technical term for such a withdrawal is **anhedonia**, which is the opposite of hedonism (excessive or unreasonable pursuits of pleasure).

Since police officers encounter depressing circumstances as an inescapable feature of their work, it is not unexpected that they develop a tendency towards anhedonic withdrawal—especially from loved ones, significant others, or family members. The technical term for the damage to personal relationships often precipitated by work stress is **medallist syndrome**. The police officer may experience a feeling of being unappreciated, taken for granted, or being misunderstood by loved ones: "Don't they realize what I've seen...what I go through?"

Enhancing one's relationships assists officers in separating the elements of their relationships from the effects of their work. Tools are provided that re-create activities and communication that were used when officers were developing their relationship with significant others—i.e., courting. Communications skills can enable police families to speak with each other at length about feelings, goals, and needs for each other. Officers should identify activities that provide pleasure for themselves and their partners.

It is, however, unfortunately the case that when police officers experience stress at work, they usually will lessen their communication of feelings and needs. They often experience a feeling of psychic fatigue that lessens the motivation to engage in pleasure-generating activities, and they may feel irritated and/or resentful. When this happens, it is precisely the time to return to the consideration, communication, and activities that originally developed the positive qualities of their relationships. Any effort to enhance the well-being of police personnel must include ways to facilitate the health and quality of officers' relationships.

4. Relaxation and Visualization Techniques
to Counteract Post-traumatic Reactions

Being aware of your body is one way to identify tension levels and reduce stress. Body awareness is something few of us is good at. When our muscles are tense, the body is telling us we are under stress. This is because the body has more adrenaline in it and more adrenaline increases skeletal muscle tension.

Body Inventory Techniques

Officers should take an inventory of their body. They should identify that they themselves are creating physical tension and that they can reduce this tension as well. Officers should learn to relax the musculature until they are practiced at controlling the levels of tension and relaxation in their body.

Whenever they are engaged in emotion-laden or frustrating encounters, officers should identify which areas of their body are experiencing tension. These will most often be the jaw, temples, neck, shoulders, or back. Simply doing this acts as a control of work encounters and the officer's body by controlling the levels of tension in these body parts while at work. The impact upon performance has often astounded those officers who have received training and departmental support in body-control techniques. Using this technique in conjunction with breathing exercises is an effective method to ensure that officers feel mentally and physically empowered and in control of the situation and themselves.

Visualization and Thought-Stopping

Behavioral therapists use visualization and thought-stopping techniques as major tools for ending obsessive and phobic thoughts. Obsessions are repetitive and intrusive trains of thought that are unrealistic, unproductive, or bring on anxiety. Phobias are specific objects or situations that make you so anxious that you avoid them. Post-traumatic images have the qualities of both obsession and phobia. For effective use of visualization and thought-stopping, the body control techniques must be practiced conscientiously throughout the day for several days.

Visualization techniques were discussed in Chapter Seven. They involve mental rehearsal activities that develop specific neural patterns and habitual activities in the brain. When officers later encounter actual threats, the brain will react reflexively in the way it has practiced. Officers will find it unnecessary to take the time and effort to consider what they will need to do to save themselves: they will just do it. For purposes of stress management, however, the technique instead uses very pleasant images and memories the officer has experienced, to be called upon when a trigger for stress is encountered.

While the size and structure of different police agencies require different application strategies for stress reduction, stress reduction is a crucial component of a wellness program. It can control and recondition the hyperarousal response, lessen the risk of psychosomatic disorder and disease, and lessen the likelihood of inappropriate reactions and behaviors by officers in the course of their work. Departments should apportion a period of time in which officers can use different elements of stress reduction as an integral and appropriate part of their work shift.

5. Action Plan for Wellness:
Psychological Debriefing and Trauma Support

What happens when officers are psychologically debriefed is that neurological activity is activated in the part of the brain that makes "sense" out of things—the cerebral cortex—after alarm or shock reactions have occurred in the officer. As you may recall, the cerebral cortex is the part of the brain where information provided by the senses is categorized and processed, and where conscious control is exerted over the officer's psychological, neurological, and physical conditions. When neurological activity is returned to the cerebral cortex after an incident, the shock reaction that the officer experienced during the incident will become less rigid, of less severity, and of shorter duration.

Pre-emptive Debriefing

In pre-emptive debriefing sessions, police officers engage in individual meetings with a debriefer who helps them recognize the signals of harmful stress reactions and prepares them for managing and defeating these negative stress reactions.

Pre-emptive debriefing counteracts the tendency for police officers to cover over destructive internal psychophysiological arousal activity in their daily lives, but does not lessen the ability for officers to maintain poise and control during encounters in the field. Each officer is given periodic debriefings every three to four months, in which the debriefer establishes an officer's experiences on and off duty, identifies those encounters which generated disturbing psychophysiological reactions in the officer, and identifies any problems in patterns of sleep, appetite, moods, activities, symptoms, and interpersonal activities that were experienced by the officer in his or her work. The debriefing is a confidential meeting: no notes are taken and no records of the encounter are made.

Once an officers' psychophysiological and work performance patterns have been identified, the debriefer and officer develop a proactive **prescriptive plan** specific to the individual officer's needs for health, well-being, and effective work performance. The plan includes stress management and reduction techniques to defuse unnecessary or inappropriate arousal. It suggests physical conditioning exercises to counteract the specific problematic reaction patterns each officer identifies. It identifies balance behaviors that are needed to counteract the impact of trigger stimuli. It generates strategies for enhancing officer well-being and effective work performance levels.

The Debriefing Technique

There are three primary purposes of psychological debriefing:

1. To *defuse* and *loosen* officers' shock reactions generated by their involvement in traumatic incidents.
2. To provide information to the officer regarding the effects of trauma upon the senses, emotions, physiology, and work performance.
3. To initiate conscious, analytic, and purposeful mental activity for effective post-incident recovery.

Through the process of psychological debriefing, conscious analysis is undertaken in which the debriefer helps the officer acknowledge the momentary, situational helplessness he or she may have experienced during a lethal encounter. In addition, the debriefer assists the officer in understanding the source of any sensory, physical, or emotional shock reactions that may have occurred during the officer's involvement in the traumatic incident. The feeling of shock, helplessness, or loss of control is especially likely to occur if the officer experienced unanticipated circumstances.

Unlike civilian techniques of crisis intervention, psychological debriefing for law enforcement personnel is not so much concerned with making the officer "feel better" as it is with preventing the "rigidification" of post-traumatic stress (or shock) reactions. It is also concerned about disruption in officer concentration or memory, impairment in decision-making, and effective use of judgment in subsequent work encounters, and aims to defuse the high levels of psychophysiological arousal that were necessary for the officer's emergency response.

While I neither intend nor desire to criticize critical incident stress-debriefing techniques used with emergency response personnel, I am concerned that psychological debriefing for police officers should be primarily individual and completely confidential. Group methods of debriefing appear problematic for police officers and should not be the only method used after major incidents. Each officer directly or peripherally involved should, wherever feasible, be individually debriefed as well as participate in ingroup efforts. There are, of course, legitimate exceptions to the above concern, such as group discussions after a catastrophic event has occurred.

The debriefing technique separates each relevant incident into five temporal stages:

1. pre-event moods and emotions
2. expectations and analyses undertaken at the point of encounter
3. impact point of the incident
4. outcome of the incident
5. aftermath of the incident

What determines the specific quality and form of post-incident stress reactions an officer develops is primarily the stage in the incident that generated a shock reaction. Shock or trauma reactions occur in officers when they experience a substantial impact that "gets through" to them—either because the incident contained unanticipated or uncontrollable elements or because the officer experienced impact from the incident even after the call was distanced in time and space.

Target Reactions

The primary target reactions for debriefing are any rigid or inflexible physical demeanor, speech pattern, or mood pattern manifest in the officer's behavior immediately after the incident. The second area of attention consists in identifying obsessive, ruminative, or excessively intense thoughts the officer has about the incident and what happened in it. Finally, debriefing examines any perceptual distortions that may have occurred during the officer's actions within the incident, so that effective post-incident restorative strategies can be made and enacted.

The debriefer aids the officer in purposefully processing those elements of the incident in which a shock reaction may have occurred. Psychological debriefing helps the officer *reframe* the incident to permit accurate perspectives for the officer and informs him or her of how hormones released during an emergency affect the senses during traumatic encounters.

Distortions in the officer's senses must be consciously processed, understood, and managed in the aftermath of traumatic incidents, for they have often contributed to an increase in the severity and duration of post-incident stress reactions. In addition, sensory distortions may have affected the officer's judgment and decision-making during the actions he or she has undertaken.

The debriefing session's technique is to "pair" questions regarding the elements of the incident and what reactions these elements initiated—i.e., "What happened and what did that make you feel?" As I have discussed earlier, when the officer identifies the feelings he or she had that were associated with each temporal element of the incident, the part of his or her brain that recognizes and processes information provided by the senses—i.e., the part that "makes sense" of the reactions the officer had (the cerebral cortex)—is activated. In this manner, shock reaction is lessened and then extinguished by the brain's "returning" neurological activity to the conscious control centers and away from the emergency, "fight or flight" centers.

1. Pre-event Moods and Emotions

It is extremely important to examine the officer's mood and what he or she was feeling or experiencing before the incident. This is because, as I have suggested, any distressed emotions, domestic difficulties, feelings of scrutiny by the department that pre-existed the incident's impact will be amplified by the trauma and increase the impact the incident would have created by itself. Then, if the officer experiences some unanticipated threat that rigidifies his or her psychophysiological reactions, the mood or emotions before the incident are likely to become intensified by the heightened arousal the officer experiences and even become fixed in the officer's subsequent life without the officer being aware of it.

Unresolved pre-incident mood patterns, irritability with a particular type of call, distressed emotions, or thoughts the officer is preoccupied with can create or exacerbate severe harm to family relationships, work performance, and/or feelings of self-worth. If police officers, for example, do not deal with beliefs that they will never see loved ones again, or see their loved ones' faces in the face of a victim, they will more likely re-experience these feelings *every time they are near the very loved ones they fear losing*. Often, these feelings cause officers to withdraw from their family but not be aware of the real reason for doing so. Indeed, the officer will most likely focus upon some currently occurring, external irritant, get angry, and then feel the need to make an exit.

As I argued earlier, the urge to withdraw from loved ones is actually a phenomenon of memory. Debriefing the pre-event elements of an incident permits the debriefer to ascertain whether officers psychologically experienced the perception of loss, threat, or harm to them or a loved one. The officer can then be made aware that such a response pattern may reoccur when they are near their significant others. Officers can be forewarned of this potential reaction, thus preventing the likelihood of distorted perceptions and/or traumatized emotions in their subsequent life and work activities.

2. Expectations and Analyses at the Point of Encounter

Debriefing of the analyses and perceptions of officers when they arrived at the scene of the incident is useful to ascertain whether officers experienced any *unanticipated* elements that caused them to react in an unplanned or unexpected manner (e.g. the officer was not able to use a pre-existing tactical plan). Clinical experience demonstrates that the "fuel" for post-incident trauma reactions exists because the officer is unable to psychologically prepare for the elements encountered in the incident—rather than the distressing nature of the incident *per se*.

During the discussion of unanticipated elements, officers may become aware of how their possible complacency, pre-judging, or expectations about what they would encounter in the contact may have disrupted their observations, strategic thinking, and tactical response. In addition, any excessive emotional and/or physical reaction officers may be experiencing subsequent to the incident may be defused by their awareness of "surprises" they experienced.

Debriefing of this temporal stage serves to prevent subsequent impulsive reactions in officer work performances—e.g., "leaping before one looks"—as well as disruptions in an officer's ability to engage in analytic thinking, concentrate, and report-writing in subsequent work encounters.

3. Impact Point of the Incident

During the debriefing, the debriefer and officer seek to identify any elements of helplessness or loss of control the officer experienced during the incident's impact. The debriefer assists the officer with understanding the causes of any sensory distortion that may have occurred during trauma. These distortions include appearances of tunnel vision, slowing of motion, detail errors, muffled sounds, etc. Such information is critical, since, as we saw in the case involving repeated contacts with a suspect at the day-care center, officers may otherwise "believe" that the inaccurate perceptions were realistic and become self-critical thereafter because they thought they had "messed up." It is in this section of the debriefing that the officer is informed of the effects of the "emergency" chemicals secreted in the brain. The purpose of this information is to prevent the officer from generating emergency levels of reaction in subsequent incidents that actually required a lesser response.

4. Outcome of the Incident

The outcome stage of debriefing helps the officer to process the emotions and judgments generated by the incident. It is during this section that the officer processes his or her fears, needs, questions, and concerns. In addition, where harm occurred to an innocent victim, the debriefer helps the officer acknowledge that he or she was just unable to impact the situation because the harm had already occurred (as in a baby not breathing) rather than believe that the harm was caused by some failure on his or her part. The officer and the debriefer identify the officer's emotional, administrative, or legal resource needs so that the officer can get the necessary support. This is the essential role of debriefing.

5. Aftermath of the Incident

There is often a period of time following a traumatic incident where post-traumatic stress reactions can occur. In a debriefing session, the debriefer aids the officer in monitoring the frequency, severity, and duration of post-traumatic reactions, and provides the defusing techniques I have talked about to prevent the development of PTSD—a syndrome that has ended many officers' careers.

Emotions are not the enemy some officers believe them to be. Of course, in ninety-eight out of a hundred calls, the officer must repress conscious awareness of any distressed emotions so that command presence is maintained. However, in the two out of a hundred calls that contain the elements of trauma, officers must use their internal emotions as *signals* to alert them to the existence of shock reaction. Then, with the use of the debriefing techniques described above, post-traumatic stress reactions can be controlled and eliminated.

Trauma Support Teams

In recognition of problems that have been experienced by having professional personnel who provide post-incident resources to officers, trauma support teams have been developed that use credible police officers (trained and supervised by a licensed professional) to perform the psychological debriefing techniques described above.

Under the direct supervision of the professional and acting as an agent of the professional, trauma support teams both protect confidentiality and apply a credible resource in the shape of a police officer who is in a position to truly communicate with, and understand, officer reactions. This is possible, of course, because these officers have experienced the same reactions and have demonstrated an effective adaptation to post-incident reactions.

Initial results during a ten-year evaluation period suggest that the effectiveness of trauma support teams is striking. Post-traumatic stress in officers debriefed by credible officers trained in psychological debriefing has been virtually eliminated. The costs of debriefing services when compared with the services provided by professionals are markedly less. Finally, there will have been a substantial reduction in the need for follow-up by a professional clinician, and there will have been *no time lost* from work by officers. In comparison, in departments in which there is either a limited debriefing resource or departmental referral to an outside resource, there has been less benefit to officers.

Trauma support is not peer counseling. It is a technique specific to the immediate aftermath of traumatic incidents.

Even when psychological services are available to officers through police agencies, there continues to be significant stigma attached to officers who request assistance for post-incident stress reactions. Further, many police officers have reported feeling "put off" or uncomfortable with the approach to the post-trauma debriefing by department psychologists. Others have found it difficult to understand how the psychologists' statements of reassurance that everything they felt was normal were going to help them extinguish severely distressing reactions they continued to feel well past the actual incident's occurrence.

In interviews with officers who had suffered psychological and/or physical injury in on-duty traumatic incidents, almost all officers reported that a great portion of the distress they experienced was due to circumstances other than just the elements of the incident itself. Obviously, a part of their concern was based upon the danger and/or death they had encountered. However, a sizeable proportion of the elements that traumatized them had occurred in the aftermath of the incident—such as questions about the adequacy of their tactical response, fears about how their co-workers and commanding officers perceived their performance, uncertainty about why their senses were strikingly altered during the incident, post-incident investigative procedures that caused them to feel they were treated like suspects, and lingering after-effects that often did not go away and began to impact ever-widening areas of their lives.

In the majority of post-incident interactions between psychologists and officers, officers are told that what they are feeling is normal. However, to the cop who has just gone through the incident, it hasn't felt normal at all. Most often, police officers claim they are "*okfine*" and fail to disclose internally occurring doubts, physical arousal, and/or distress. As we have seen, this failure to disclose is logical, given the historical tradition of police officers repressing overt expression or disclosure of painful emotions and/or doubts about the adequacy of their tactical response.

Thus, the officer is caught in a bind. He or she does not feel fine, is inhibited from talking to a professional who can help, and feels external pressure that can create secondary trauma. For example, the emphasis in post-incident investigative procedures is upon the finding of facts, and the officer is interviewed to discuss the incident in detail. Where a police association or legal representation is mobilized, the officer is most often advised against making any statements regarding his or her involvement in the incident.

What course of action is the proper one for the officer? If he or she does not give a statement, the department may see him or her as possibly guilty of some wrongdoing. The department may feel the officer has something to hide. If the officer gives a statement, however, he or she may be liable for subsequent legal action against them.

Secondary trauma to officers can be created by inconsistency between a department's policy and individual supervisors' beliefs in defining what incident types are sufficiently traumatic to require post-trauma debriefing support, as well as by how the department responds procedurally to these incidents. In most police departments, only the officer who has discharged his or her weapon at a suspect and has struck that suspect has been provided with post-incident support services. Officers who have experienced encounters with death to children, drowning, fires, fatal traffic collisions where innocent people have been killed for no purpose or reason, officers in officer-involved shootings who were not in a tactical position to discharge their weapon (while another officer did), and officers who discharged their weapon but failed to strike the suspect—all have very often been expected to handle trauma and get back to work with no disruption.

Where a department has not followed uniform response procedures to life-threatening contacts, there have been unpredictable, inconsistent, and, at times, damaging actions resulting in unnecessary trauma to involved officers.

The trauma support team provides immediate and on-scene resource for the officer (or dispatcher) who has encountered incidents included in the criteria for trauma support. Rather than limiting its resources to officer-involved shootings only, the team should respond to all types of incidents that have the characteristics of trauma.

If using wellness and trauma support tools and resources can save one officer, aren't they worth it? These techniques have been proven. They maintain officers' effective control of their thoughts, emotions, and actions under conditions of stress, pressure, and emergency. I thoroughly recommend all officers to use them. They can save your life.

Bibliography

Ametz, B., B. Fjellner, P. Eneroth, & A. Kallner 1986. "Neuro-endocrine response selectivity to standardized psychological stressors." **International Journal of Psychosomatics**, 33, 19–27.

Averill, J. 1973. "Personal control over aversive stimuli and its relationship to stress." **Psychological Bulletin**, 80, 286–307.

Axelrod, J., & T. Reisine 1984. "Stress hormones." **Science**, 224, 452–459.

Bandura, A. 1977. "Self-efficacy." **Psychological Review**, 84, 191–215.

———. 1982a. "Self-efficacy mechanism in human agency." **American Psychologist**, 37 (2), 122–147.

———. 1982b. "The self and mechanisms of agency." *Psychological Perspectives on the Self,* edited by J. Suls, 3–39. Hillsdale, NJ: Erlbaum.

Bardzik, Jeffrey, Sergeant, Orange County Sheriff's Department, Supervising Sergeant and Tactics Instructor, Orange County Sheriff's Academy, personal communication, 1999.

Blum, L. 1994. Final report, results of the research, Milwaukee Police Association Interest Arbitration Hearings.

———. 1998. "Incidence and prevalence of work stress." International Union of Police Associations National Study.

———. 1999. "The impact of public safety work upon the health and life of those who serve: disease, disturbance, disability, and mortality in Washington State public safety personnel." Report to the Joint Committee on Retirement Legislation, Washington State Councils of Fire Fighters and Police Officers.

Brod, J. 1959. "Circulatory changes underlying blood pressure elevation during acute emotional stress in normotensive and hypertensive situations." **Clinical Science**, 18, 169–270.

———. 1971. "The influence of higher nervous processes induced by psychosocial environment on the development of essential hypertension." *Stress, Society and Disease,* edited by L. Levi, pp. 312–323. New York: Oxford University Press.

Cannon, W.B. 1929. *Bodily changes in pain, fear, hunger, and rage.* New York: Appleton.

Cannon-Bowers, J. & E. Salas, eds. 1988. *Making Decisions Under Stress: Implications for Individual and Team Training.*Washington D.C.: American Psychological Association Press.

The Diagnostic and Statistical Manual-III-Revised. Washington, DC: American Psychiatric Association, 1987.

Deuel, Edward, Sergeant, Huntington Beach Police Department, expert on officer survival, personal communication, 1999.

Ellis, A. 1973. *Humanistic Psychology: The Rational-emotive Approach.* New York: Julian.

Engel, G.L. 1971. "Sudden and rapid death during psychological distress." **Annals of Internal Medicine**, 74, 771–782.

Everly, G.S. 1986. "A biopsychosocial analysis of psychosomatic disease." *Contemporary Directions in Psychopathology,* ed. T. Millom & G. Klerman, pp. 535–551. New York: Guilford.

———. 1989. *A Clinical Guide to the Treatment of the Human Stress Response.* New York: Plenum.

Everly, G.S., & H. Benson, 1988. "Disorders of arousal and the relaxation response: A reformulation of the nature and treatment of stress-related disease." Paper presented to IV International Conference on Psychophysiology, Prague, Czechoslovakia.

Everly, G.S., & R. Rosenfeld, 1981. *The Nature and Treatment of the Stress Response.* New York: Plenum.

Everly, G.S., S. Shapiro, S. Levine, E. Newman, & M. Sherman, 1987. "An investigation into the relationships between personality and clinical syndromes." *Proceedings of the Conference on the Millon Clinical Inventories* ed. C. Green. Minneapolis: NCS.

Everly, G.S., & K. Smith, 1987. "Occupational stress and its management." *Human Stress: Current Selected Research, Vol. 2,* ed. J. Humphrey. New York: AMS.

Everly, G.S., & S.H. Sobelman, 1987. *The Assessment of the Human Stress Response: Neurological, Biochemical, and Psychological Foundations.* New York: AMS.

Federal Bureau of Investigation, 1992. *Killed in the Line of Duty: A Study of Selected Felonious Killings of Law Enforcement Officers.* Washington, DC: U.S. Department of Justice.

Fell, R.D., W.C. Richard, & W.L. Wallace, 1980. "Psychological job stress and the police officer." **Journal of Police Science and Administration**, 8, 139–144.

Frankenhaeuser, M. 1981. "Coping with stress at work." **International Journal of Health Services**, 11, 491–510.

————. 1986. "A psychobiological framework for research on human stress and coping." *Dynamics of Stress: Physiological, Psychological and Social Perspectives* ed. Mortimer H. Appley and Richard Trumbell, pp. 101–116. New York: Plenum.

Frankenhaeuser, M., U. Lundberg, & L. Forsman, 1980. "Dissociation between sympathetic-adrenal and pituitary-adrenal responses to an achievement situation characterized by high controllability: comparison between Type A and Type B males and females." **Biological Psychology**, 10, 79–91.

Froberg, J. C. Karlsson, L. Levi, & L. Lidberg, 1971. "Physiological and biochemical stress reactions induced by psychosocial stimuli." *Society, Stress and Disease* ed. L. Levi, pp. 280–295. New York: Oxford University Press.

Garfield, C. 1984. *Peak Performance,* New York: Warner Books. 1984.

Gellhorn, E. 1968. "Central nervous system tuning and its implications for neuropsychiatry." **Journal of Nervous and Mental Disease**, 147, 148–162.

Girdano, D., & G. Everly, 1986. *Controlling Stress and Tension.* 2nd ed. Englewood Cliffs, NJ: Prentice-Hall.

Gray, J. 1985. "Issues in the neuropsychology of anxiety." *Anxiety and Anxiety Disorders* ed. A. Tuma and J. Maser, pp. 5–26. Hillsdale, NJ: Erlbaum.

Heal, C. "Sid" 2000. *Sound Doctrine: A Tactical Primer.* New York: Lantern Books.

Henry, J.P., & P. Stephens, 1977. *Stress, Health, and the Social Environment.* New York: Springer-Verlag.

Johansson, G., & P.O. Sanden, 1982. *Mental belastning och arbetstillfredsstallelse kontrollrumsarbete. (Mental load and job satisfaction of control room operators.)* (Rep. No.40). Stockholm: University of Stockholm, Department of Psychology.

Karasek, R.A. 1979. "Job demands, job decision latitude, and mental strain: Implications for job redesign." **Administrative Science Quarterly**, 24, 285–307.

Kozlowski, Steve. 1998 "Training and Developing Adaptive Teams: Theory, Principles, and Research." Cannon-Bowers & Salas, *Making Decisions Under Stress: Implications for Individual and Team Training*, Washington D.C.: American Psychological Association Press.

Krantz, D.S. 1980. "Cognitive processes and recovery from heart attack: A review and theoretical analysis." **Journal of Human Stress**, September, 27–38.

Lazarus, R. S. 1966a. *Psychological stress and the coping process.* New York: McGraw-Hill.

———. 1966b. *Stress and coping.* New York: McGraw-Hill.

———. 1982. "Thoughts on the relations between cognitions and emotions." **American Psychologist**, 37, 1019–1024.

Lazarus, R.S., & S. Folkman, 1984. *Stress, Appraisal, and Coping.* New York: Springer.

LEOKA Study, "Law Enforcement Officers Killed and Assaulted in the Line of Duty, 1990–1994." California Commission on Police Officer Standards and Training, Final Report, 1996.

Lundberg, U., & L. Forsman, 1979. "Adrenal-medullary and adrenal-cortical responses to understimulation and overstimulation: comparison between Type A and Type B persons." **Biological Psychology**, 9, 79–89.

Lundberg, U., & M. Frankenhaeuser, 1980. "Pituitary-adrenal and sympathetic-adrenal correlates of distress and effort." **Journal of Psychosomatic Research**, 24, 125–130.

McCabe, P., & N. Schneiderman, 1984. "Psychophysiologic reactions to stress." *Behavioral Medicine* ed. N. Schneiderman & J. Tapp. Hillsdale, NJ: Erlbaum.

Meichenbaum, D. 1977. *Cognitive Behavior Modification*. New York: Plenum.

Meichenbaum, D., & M. Jaremko, 1983. *Stress Reduction and Prevention*. New York: Plenum.

Miller, Ronald K., Sergeant, Huntington Beach Police Department, Special Weapons and Tactics Team Supervising Sergeant, Supervisor of Training Unit, expert on special weapons and tactics, personal communication, 1999.

Mitchell, J. 1984. "High tension: Keeping stress under control." **Firehouse**, 86–90.

Osuna, Felix, Lieutenant, Santa Ana Police Department, Commander, Special Weapons and Tactics Unit, expert on officer survival and officer tactics, personal communication, 1999.

Pitman, R.K. 1988. "Post-traumatic stress disorder, conditioning, and network theory." **Psychiatric Annals**, 18, 182–189.

———. 1989. "Post-traumatic stress disorder, hormones, and memory." **Biological Psychiatry**, 50, 450–452.

Seligman, M.E.P. 1975. *Helplessness: On Depression, Development and Death*. San Francisco: Freeman.

Selye, H. 1981. "Police stress." **Police Stress Magazine**, 1, 1–3.

Stratton, J.G., D.A. Parker & J.R. Snibbe, 1984. "Post-traumatic stress: Study of police officers involved in shootings." **Psychological Reports**, 127–131.

Theorell, T., E. Lind, U. Lundberg, T. Christensson, & O. Edhag, 1981. "The individual and his work in relation to myocardial infraction." *Society, Stress and Disease. Vol IV: Working Life* ed. L. Levi. New York: Oxford.

Thompson, S.C. 1981. "Will it hurt less if I can control it? A complex answer to a simple question." **Psychological Bulletin**, 90(1), 89–101.

Unestahl, Lars-Eric, 1976. in Garfield, 1984.

———. 1979. "Hypnotic Preparation of Athletes." Paper published at the Department of Sport Psychology, Orebro University, Sweden.

Urwin, H., E. Baade, & S. Levine, 1978. *Psychobiology of Stress: A Study of Coping Men.* New York: Academic Press.

Violanti, J.M., J.E. Vena, & J.R. Marshall, 1986. "Disease risk and mortality among police officers: New evidence and contributing factors." **Journal of Police Science and Administration,** 14, 17–23.

Wemmer, Richard, Captain, Los Angeles Police Department, Commander, Los Angeles Police Academy, producer of many videotape re-enactments of officer-involved shootings and murdered police officers, expert on officer tactics, officer safety, officer survival, personal communication, 1999.